DEAD ON TIME

DEAD ON TIME

THE MEMOIR OF AN SOE AND OSS AGENT IN OCCUPIED FRANCE

JEAN CLAUDE GUIET

The
History
Press

Unless otherwise stated, all images are courtesy of the Claudia
Holzer archives

First published 2016

The History Press
The Mill, Brimscombe Port
Stroud, Gloucestershire, GL5 2QG
www.thehistorypress.co.uk

British Library Cataloguing in Publication Data.
A catalogue record for this book is available from the British Library.

ISBN 978 0 7509 6526 2

Typesetting and origination by The History Press
Printed and bound in Great Britain by TJ International Ltd

CONTENTS

FOREWORD BY
ROBERT MALOUBIER

One day in May 1944, in London, our boss Major Charles Staunton told Violette Szabó, the 'courier' of our team, and myself:

> The radio operator who is going to join us is a very young American, born of French parents, a tenderfoot, named Jean Claude Guiet. An OSS issue, he has been trained in the States. They have Special Training Schools similar to ours in the UK, you know. I suggest we have lunch together at Rose, the French restaurant in Soho, tomorrow. You know the place, don't you?

Charles is the boss of our Special Operations Executive (SOE) team, 'Salesman'. He has been on three secret assignments in occupied France. Captured by Vichy police in 1941, he had managed to escape across the Pyrénées to Spain, Portugal and back to England. A former international press correspondent, he is shrewd. The perfect boss and spiritual father for a youngster like me. I spent seven months as a saboteur under his command behind Normandy's Atlantic Wall in 1943. We were flown back to the UK in February aboard a small plane of SOE's Moonlight Squadron.

Rose is a typical bistro of Soho, a cosmopolitan district of London. A sort of narrow corridor invaded by kitchen smokes. Crude marble tables, thick earthenware plates. Nonetheless, Rose provides thick juicy steaks, and buckets of crisp chips. The bistro is unlicensed, so guests go and get their fill of thick red wine next door, at the York Minster, Dean Street's famed French pub. His landlord, the Belgian Victor Berlemont, boasts London's widest moustache: 'ten inches from wing tip to wing tip'!

Jean Claude Guiet is dead on time. Impeccably clad in officer's 'pinks', tall, sporty, handsome. Open face, frank grey eyes.

Violette whispers in my ear, 'A good looker, isn't he?'

Jean Claude sips his wine bravely, keeps wolfing his steak down. Mischievously, Violette stops him short. 'It's horse meat, you know! In the UK, meat is rationed, meat of all origins, but horse meat ...' Knowing how Yanks revere their horses, 'the noblest conquest of men', she expected him to choke. The lad is unruffled.

'So, welcome to the club,' says Violette. 'Now tell us more about yourself.'

Jean Claude was born in the Jura region of France, close to the Swiss border. His parents, both professors, settled later in the United States. In June 1940, he was holidaying in France with his elder brother when both were nearly caught by the Germans who had invaded the country. They managed to reach Spain, Portugal and thereafter board a New York-bound steamship. He was approaching graduation from Harvard when Hirohito hit Pearl Harbor. He decided to join the armed forces. There a talent scout noted that he spoke perfect French. The OSS took over. At Camp X, he qualified as a potential secret agent to infiltrate occupied France and was transferred to SOE's 'Baker Street Irregulars'.

'From now on, you're one of ours,' Violette tells him.

Bi-national, born of a French mother and an English father, 'Vi' is a 23-year-old war widow, and the mother of 2-year-old Tania, who often babbles at her side. Her husband, a French *legionnaire*, had been killed at El Alamein. He had never set eyes on his daughter. Violette had conceived an irrepressible hatred for the

Germans who had killed 'the man of her life'. She had joined the Forces. Spotted as multilingual, she had been 'invited' to join SOE's French Section.

We are members of a team just as close-knit as a bomber crew, going to the cinema together, spending dinner-and-dance evenings at our favourite Knightsbridge Studio Club, playing poker or pontoon – a variation on Black Jack – at Wimpole Street's SOE 'hostel'.

We were to parachute early June into a communist *maquis* group in Limousin, central France. Staunton was to assess its fighting strength, its will to fight and see that it was properly supplied with weapons and equipment to be dropped from England. I was to train its men in guerrilla warfare, lead groups of them to road and rail ambushes, organise air drops and sabotage roads and railroads. Jean Claude was to be in charge of radio transmissions, Vi was to liaise with nearby SOE networks.

In early June 1944 we made for Hazells Hall, a stately Edwardian manor nested in a huge and elegant park in Cambridgeshire, one of the French Section 'departing stations'. We made two or three aborted attempts. On the eve of 6 June, our B-24 four-engine Liberator bomber took off for good. We played poker throughout the three- or four-hour flight to Limoges. Alas, above our assigned dropping zone, the captain came to us: 'Sorry, lady and gentlemen. The reception committee that was to welcome you is missing. See for yourself: no lights on the ground! My orders are clear: I am not to drop you blind! Here we go, back to UK ...'

Using our 'chutes as a pillow, we lay down on the bomb compartment floor and fell asleep. From time to time I woke up, paid a visit to the cockpit, had a chat with the crew, looked out to dense cloud. Through gaps in the thick clouds one could see a foamy sea ripped by ship's wakes. I wondered loudly, 'What are they?'

'Well, ships' wakes mean that a convoy is passing by across the Channel,' replied the captain. 'That's all.'

Past dawn we touched down at Tempsford, our Moonlight Squadron airbase. A car took us back to Hazells Hall. A few minutes later, we were fast asleep.

Around noon a hullaballoo woke me up. The bar was seemingly going wild with merrymakers bursting with laughter, crying out with joy, yelling and singing their heads off as if they had been drinking the night through. The beaming batman who brought a cup of tea a few minutes later spelt the news: 'It's D Day gentlemen. "We" have landed this morning!'

So that explained why the Channel was rippled by the wakes of a convoy, one amounting to 5,000 vessels landing 140,000 men on the beaches of Normandy!

We parachuted on the night of 7 June. Jean Claude tapped a safe arrival message out to London.

Two days later, disaster struck: Violette, sent by Staunton to liaise with the head of a nearby SOE network, ran into the vanguard of the ravenous SS Panzer Division *Das Reich*, which had been ordered by Rommel to leave its station in southern France and help contain Normandy's beachhead. She was captured. We were never to see her again.

Though we were grieving, there was a war to be won. So Jean Claude went on dispatching hundreds of messages and eventually joined me in ambushing enemy convoys. Months later, Limoges' German garrison surrendered. We drove to Paris. Jean Claude was most welcome at my family's home in Neuilly, a northwestern suburb of Paris. Soon after, he was called back to the States.

I enlisted with Force 136, SOE's Far East branch and was posted to Calcutta. Jean Claude joined a similar section of the OSS, based in Kunming, China. We managed, I don't know how, to exchange letters across the Himalayas. In one of these he humorously described the mess that was the so-called 'indomitable' Chinese army. Alas, the letter was scrutinised by OSS censorship and poor Jean Claude was to be tried by a court martial for defaming America's Great Ally! By a stroke of luck – thanks to Japan's surrender! – the court martial was suspended and Jean Claude was discharged from the army and set free to resume his studies at Harvard.

Thereafter we lost sight of each other for nearly forty years, until a resident of Wormelow, a village near Hereford where Vi had spent some holidays, founded a museum dedicated to her. The event being highly publicised, Jean Claude and I were invited to attend. After a forty-year gap, the 'youngster' had not changed much. Hair thinning, but not an extra pound of fat on him. His straightforward look and sense of humour were still there. It was a happy reunion. Later we met again in Paris and Lons-le-Saunier, where he had a family home.

Thanks to his memoirs, anyone can now learn about the adventures of an American 'tenderfoot' fighting for the liberation of France and getting through, all smiles.

Thank you, Jean Claude!

Bob Maloubier

FOREWORD BY
TANIA SZABÓ

Jean Claude Guiet, half-French, half-American, was a quiet man, self-contained and a tower of strength within a medium frame. He had proved his supreme suitability to be an SOE operative. On the occasions that I met him I was struck by his stillness, quickness and understanding of tight security – characteristics essential to the war-time wireless operator.

He tells his story without arrogance and self-aggrandisement – it is a simple tale of a simple man who accomplished his tasks superbly well under the most dangerous of circumstances. His irritation at lack of security, or transmissions that were far too long – and thus perilous – was well known.

He was born, educated and lived in France as a youngster and then in the US. This background was perfect for the tasks set him not only during those war years but in the post-war years until his retirement, where he sought excitement his own way, but always in control with his outwardly reserved and instinctively careful nature.

He admired and was somewhat smitten by Violette Szabó GC, CdeG★, my mother and fellow SOE agent, when they met in

London to prepare for their June 1944 mission in the Haute Vienne, 'Salesman II'. His team, made up of Philippe Liewer aka Major Charles Staunton, Bob Maloubier aka Bob Mortier and Violette aka Louise, were quartered in Sussac while Jean Claude remained alone and concealed in a small rural house near a watermill with his wireless equipment. Violette was captured after a gunfight with an advance unit of the Panzer Division *Das Reich*, 'Der Führer', so it fell to Jean Claude to send and receive 'a flurry of transmissions concerning her capture' under very dangerous circumstances.

It was very much my pleasure and honour to have met him and spoken with him. With great kindness he wrote the introduction to the 2007 hardback edition of *Young, Brave and Beautiful*, my account of Violette's two missions of 1944, in the second of which Jean Claude played such an important role.

Violette was clearly drawn to him as, pushing her bike, she accompanied him to his little house while they chatted about their mission and got to know one another. So, thank you from the heart, Claude, for providing a sense of stability and thoughtfulness to Violette on the eve of that fateful day.

Tania Szabó

FOREWORD BY
CLAUDIA ALICE HOLZER

Jean Claude Guiet's parents, René Georges Guiet and Jeanne Zelie Seigneur, were married on 26 May 1920 in Urbana, Illinois. His parents both took guest professorships in French at the University of Illinois in Urbana in 1921. Jean Claude's older brother, Pierre, was born in Urbana the same year. In 1923, the family returned to Belfort, France, where Jean Claude was born on 24 March 1924. In 1925, the family immigrated to the US and settled in Northampton, Massachusetts.

Jean Claude's father, René, had been born in Laval, France, in 1896. He was a graduate of the French military college at Saint-Cyr and served in the First World War, earning the Croix de Guerre for exceptional conduct. He also received a Bachelor's and PhD from the Sorbonne. His doctoral thesis dealt with opera libretti in France from Gluck to the French Revolution. He taught at the University of Illinois and Hunter College before joining the faculty at Smith College in 1926. Smith College is one of the so-called Seven Sisters, seven highly ranked colleges for women comparable to the Ivy League colleges. René was a well-respected professor emeritus of French language and literature and Chairman of the French Department for decades. He was an accomplished violinist and played in the Smith College orchestra. As a child, Jean Claude also played the violin.

Jean Claude's mother, Jeanne, was born in Mandeure, western France in 1896. She was a respected assistant professor emeritus of French, also at Smith College. She was a master gardener and worked tirelessly on her flower beds. She also was a legendary hostess who employed an excellent chef, who happened to be her sister, Claire Seigneur.

In 1926, Jean Claude's parents bought a beautiful house that had been built in 1857 at 70 Washington Avenue. It had extensive gardens which were Jeanne's pride and joy. Jean Claude's parents entertained with lavish formal dinner parties in the best French tradition. Their house was furnished with gorgeous French and American antiques, and oriental rugs of the finest quality graced their floors. It was truly exquisite. This is the world in which Jean Claude spent most of his childhood, except for summers in France. Jeanne demanded that only French be spoken at home.

Jean Claude's childhood was sheltered and culturally very different from the informal American ways, which made him feel out of the norm. René was distant and intellectual. He believed that children should be seen and not heard. Jeanne was domineering, difficult, demanding and tough. To her, appearances were of paramount importance and she gleaned much pleasure from the beautiful objects surrounding her, much more than from people. She was emotionally distant and Jean Claude worked hard to please her, even though it was clear that Pierre was her favourite. Sadly, trying to please his mother was a driving force through much of his life. He had a close relationship with Pierre, his older brother and his only playmate. It is no wonder that, by his own admission, his overly sheltered childhood 'resulted in a weak development of self-confidence'. He was timid and nervous in interactions outside his family and had an astounding lack of knowledge of the world around him.

Thankfully for Jean Claude, the family summered in France in the Jura village of Conliège. The woman Jean Claude referred to as his Grandmama, Marte Beley, was grandmother in name only, but he loved her very much and she was a wonderful influence on him. Jean Claude had a close connection to her and he truly enjoyed his summers with her. She allowed him to be a boy, to get his clothes dirty and to play and laugh. He worked alongside the farmers, learning how to harvest hay and a variety of other chores such as churning butter, making cheese, killing and plucking chickens, chopping wood and building fences from tree branches. Jean Claude's mother was not pleased that he was acting like a 'peasant', but his Grandmama prevailed saying that she needed these chores to be done, thus liberating Jean Claude from his mother for a few short months. He loved to ride his bicycle and explore the countryside in complete freedom. Working the land remained a pleasure in Jean Claude's life.

In the summer of 1939, only Pierre and Jean Claude made the trip to France. With Hitler threatening invasion, they spent an unsettled summer helping their Grandmama stock up on provisions. Pierre had a US passport since he was born there. But being the son of two French citizens made him a French citizen too. He had also turned 18 the previous February. Under French law, that made him eligible for the French army draft. Jean Claude was not affected since he was too young. René and Jeanne tried to straighten out the situation from the US, but realised that it would take time. Stuck in France, Pierre and Jean Claude were enrolled in the *lycée* in Lons-le-Saunier. Finally, Pierre received a French passport and a travel visa to Spain. They managed to flee to Lisbon, and in September 1940, they sailed on the ship *Excalibur* to New Jersey, where their parents met them.

The family spent that night with Tante Margot (Jeanne's sister) and Oncle Lorenzo Marchini, who had a lovely apartment in New York City. Jean Claude had a good relationship with Margot and Lorenzo and he stayed with them whenever he was in town. The family returned to Northampton, Massachusetts, and Jean Claude attended Deerfield Academy for the next two and a half years.

He entered Harvard University in 1942 but was immature and did little work in his first year. He lived in Dunster House and recalled lining up peas on the end of a knife and flicking them at some unsuspecting housemate. Maturity would come later! It was a relief to him when he received his draft notice since he was worried he was about to be kicked out of Harvard for low grades. He entered the US Army in June of 1943. Aged 19, he was an immature, naïve, privileged and innocent young man. He had completed most of his basic training when it was 'discovered' that he was French-born and a native French speaker. As a result, he was evaluated and assigned to SOE/OSS. He took his training seriously but admitted that the non-regimented life in SOE/OSS was much more to his liking than the highly organised regular military. His training and wartime experiences shaped the man he would become. He developed a strong sense of duty and responsibility. When he was discharged, he was much more ready and capable of dealing with the realities of civilian life.

Claudia Holzer

PREFACE BY
JEAN CLAUDE GUIET

On my seventieth birthday I received a computer. My experience with them had been limited to studying the output of mainframe units, and the reality of hands-on working with one was an entirely new and frustrating experience. With the help of my children and grandchildren, as well as *Word for Dummies*, I have managed to master enough of the operational complexities to feel sufficiently competent to try writing. Naturally, at my age, when one reaches what Disraeli called one's anecdotage, the first thing that one feels comfortable with is one's memoirs.

The fiftieth anniversary of the end of the Second World War, with its heightened interest in that conflict, motivated a long-dormant realisation that I should perhaps relate my experiences during the war (not that they represented anything much out of the ordinary from the myriad activities that occurred throughout it). Indeed, my experiences are of interest in part because of the popularity and hype of James Bond Syndrome and the fact that I was involved in an operation in which the outstanding importance was the actions and fate of our courier, one of three women who were the only agents in the Secret Operations Executive (SOE) to have been awarded the George Cross. For me, the importance and particular personal interest lies in the operation's relative ease, enjoyment and lack of contention compared to the norm for that war. Ben Bradlee summarised one aspect of it perfectly in his 1995 book *A Good Life: Newspapering and Other Adventures*: the war had been 'more exciting, more meaningful than anything I'd ever done. This is why I had such a wonderful time in the war. I just plain loved it. Loved the excitement, even loved being a little bit scared. Loved the sense of achievement, even if it was only getting from Point A to Point B, loved the camaraderie.'

Right after my discharge in November 1945, until the reality of the needs of starting civilian life took over, I had toyed with the idea of writing a memoir of my adventures. In the short time before returning to college, I had even filled an exam book with notes that might serve as an aide-mémoire. Rediscovery of that exam book, which had survived many moves, contributed greatly to my decision to go ahead with the project even though its data often turned out to be incomplete because I had too often omitted dates, names and place names, probably on the assumption they would never be forgotten. Yet the sequence of events was still there and the few details that were recorded helped jog my memory on to many more memories, reinforcing the realisation that many details would be more difficult to recall or trace the longer I waited. There are still many specifics and fairly important events about which I have no clear memory other than the fact they happened.

I have undertaken this effort somewhat as a challenge and for my personal satisfaction with, perhaps, an undercurrent of recording my experiences for family posterity should anyone be interested. I may well have had the desire to add my 'two cents' worth' to the war tales of the early post-war period and current fiftieth anniversary though, in fact, most seemed to be more moving and interesting than mine, as were many of the accounts I have heard from other veterans. From all of these sources I realised that my army experiences, combat and other, had none of the regimented group discipline of the regular combat units or the extended exposure to the many horrors – weather, tedium, fatigue, exhaustion, and all the other battle dangers – of participants in the Pacific operations, the Italian campaign, D-Day or the Ardennes. I can only invoke and apply the view of Teddy Roosevelt: I had a relatively 'lovely little war'.

DEAD ON TIME
THE MEMOIR

CHAPTER I

My introduction to the war came well before my direct involvement in it, when my brother Pierre, three years my senior, and I happened to be in France when war was declared on 3 September 1939. As we quite regularly had done in previous years, we had come over in June on the *Normandie*. For the first time we had made the trip alone without our parents, a major event in itself in our lives. I was fifteen with no experience of life outside a protective first-generation French family. My brother, at least, had experienced being away from home at school.

We spent a pleasant early summer in the Jura with our grandmother in her large house and garden in a small farming village where the cows followed a cowherd out in the morning and returned with him in the evening. Each cow returned on its own into its stable. The milk was taken straight to a cooperative and sold retail as well as wholesale immediately, refrigeration being non-existent. It was a daily meeting place. Other than dairy and some agriculture, the vineyards and winemaking were the primary village activity. It was a peaceful existence with weekly trips to the nearest city for the weekly Thursday *marché*.

As war became imminent we ran into our first difficulties when we went to Lyon to get the necessary visas for the return to America. Being fifteen I had no problem at all obtaining an exit visa on my French passport: Pierre, however, though born of French parents in Urbana, Illinois, and therefore an American citizen by birth, could not obtain a French exit visa on his US passport. By French law, being born of French parents he was French and, being eighteen, he was eligible for the draft. It was reluctantly decided after much correspondence that we would remain in France and attend the *lycée* while our parents worked on the problem and pulled strings from the United States. In retrospect, a great deal of faith was obviously being placed in the reputation of the French army.

We spent a difficult six months in the very unfamiliar environment of the French educational system, where in almost every subject our classmates were way ahead of us. My two years of Latin (translation of Latin to English) were faced with their four years (translation of Latin to French and French to Latin); they were starting a third year of geometry and a first year of algebra versus my one year of algebra and no geometry; while I could speak and read French fluently, I had no experience in writing it, and in the twice weekly *dictée* my fellow students' neatness (underlining the title twice without crossing any part of a letter that projected below the line, and accomplishing the entire dictation accurately in ink without corrections) was beyond me. Never did I miss pencil and eraser so much.

The exit visa problem was finally resolved early in the spring on the advice of a family friend. It was a simple, if somewhat irregular solution, and perhaps typical of a country that came up with the adage that laws are made to be bypassed. Pierre was to obtain a French passport from a different Prefecture without making any mention of the US passport. It was astonishingly simple in those pre-computer days, and in late April he had a French passport with an exit visa to visit Spain with no more than an admonition to keep in contact for possible call up. Since there were no other visas on this French passport he was, it was thought, limited to travel in Spain. Our plans were obviously quite different: once into Spain, Pierre would destroy his French passport and proceed under the American passport. By April everything seemed to be in place and just before the beginning of the debacle, Mother had made boat reservations for us, but events overtook us.

There was a growing uncertainty that all was well and we had felt somewhat uncomfortable with the apparent hesitancy on both sides of what came to be called 'the phony war'. The photo in *Life* magazine showing a French soldier on guard sitting on a chair with his feet in slippers in front of one of the fortress doors in the rear of the Maginot Line (in retrospect) epitomized the situation. Throughout that winter we had wondered, as did many others, what was really happening. Listening to French radio broadcasts, which began with eight catchy notes from *Auf der Luneburger Heide*, did little to enlighten us. Pervasive among the population was a considerable apathy, almost passivity, and not much confidence in official government war communiqués.

We continued to ride our bikes every day except Sunday, cycling the five kilometers to the *lycée* in Lons-le-Saunier, past the barracks where the Moroccan troops seemed to do nothing but stand around, and our only other contact with the reality of the war occurred when several companies of reservists were quartered in our village and in our garage with a mobile field kitchen in back in a courtyard. The soldiers slept on straw and hay and used their overcoats for blankets. Their equipment was old, 1918 Lebel rifles with long, thin bayonets that looked more like fencing foils than lethal weapons, and they left them lying casually about. They, too, wandered about the village with bits of straw and hay on their uniforms doing nothing during the two weeks of their stay and, while we enjoyed watching the preparation and distribution of the meals in the mobile field kitchen, even our youthful enthusiasm did not succeed in impressing us with any of the 'military might' we were witnessing. Our only participative war effort involved us in an informal group keeping an ineffective and disorganized lookout for enemy paratroopers (for which the French army provided us with cigarettes). It was with this encouragement that as a teenager wanting to act adult I started to smoke in earnest.

The reality of the situation (which we had seriously begun to suspect with the change in command from General Gamelin to General Weygand) became a strong, almost impossible-to-deny certainty by the middle of May, when the first refugees started passing through town. It really hit home hard on 13 June, when we were all abruptly, and with no specific explanation, sent home from school and told the *lycée* would be closed until further notice. The very next day some distant cousins, who were being relocated by the Peugeot factory to near Saint-Étienne in central France, stopped by and brought with them a sense of urgency and fear. We started to get the old Renault ready and agreed to take our neighbor's son Dédé (who was a little younger than I) and daughter Mimi (who was probably seventeen) with us. This made five of us with grandmother, who kept insisting she was responsible for us and had to come.

At about 4:00 a.m. on the fifteenth we were awakened by tremendous detonations which rattled the windows. With a sense of adventure, Pierre and I hastened cautiously to town on our bikes to find out what was happening. The gasoline storage tanks in Lons had been blown up to keep them from the Germans. The town was in pandemonium; the narrow streets were noisy and more crowded than on market day with an excited melee of evacuees from the north trying to get through and locals getting ready to leave. Military vehicles of all sorts added to the confusion. In a very short time there was near gridlock.

We hurried home appalled, and it was quickly decided that it was time we should leave. I cannot remember any specific reasons why we made the decision, but excitement, stress and the element of public panic was obviously involved. It just seemed like the thing to do. We managed to strap two mattresses, blankets and suitcases on the roof of the car; stuffed food and sandwiches as well as two cans of gasoline in the small trunk; and left shortly after noon with no more specific destination in mind than heading south.

Our experience with gridlock in Lons that morning kept us on back roads, bypassing all big towns whenever possible. That afternoon we got south of Lyon and stopped at the edge of a wheat field to camp for the night. The farmer came down, worried that we might damage his field, but when he saw we were careful people he kindly offered to rent a room for the women and let the boys sleep on hay in a shed.

The next day we got through Saint-Étienne and into true refugee traffic. While the traffic north of Saint-Étienne had been acceptable thanks to the back roads, we were now limited to main roads through the very mountainous Massif Central. Overloaded cars and trucks struggled to crawl up the steep, curving road; radiators overheated, trucks overturned at sharp turns on the very concave Route Nationale, and there were frequent pileups caused by frantic drivers trying to get past anything they perceived as an obstacle delaying their progress. We finally reached Le Puy in the Haute Loire department, stressed, tired and somewhat shaken and wondering if we had done the right thing. We had been told by some northern refugees that we could find places to sleep there, but everything was full. We finally found a barn we could stay in, on our mattresses and the hay. We had planned to go further south, but spent the next day there, too, both because it was raining hard and because the radio was mentioning the possibility of an armistice and urging everyone to stay where they were. So we continued our search for housing.

Luckily, we found a place in a large farm outside the village of Sanssac l'Église. In addition to the barn, the outbuildings and the usual enormous manure pile, the farmhouse was a large two-story building that at one time had been a small manorial holding.

Immediately upon our arrival, even before showing us what she had to offer in terms of lodgings, the farmer's wife invited us in for a snack (*le gouté*). We must have looked very much in need. As we entered the enormous kitchen, she shooed chickens off the table and pushed two sheep back outside. Poor grandmother, who was neat and clean to the point of extreme fastidiousness, was obviously disconcerted. The plates, however, were clean and the fresh, homemade wholewheat bread with unsalted butter that had been churned just that morning, homemade sausage, and cheese were deliciously satisfying, most welcome, and thoroughly enjoyed.

The room available for us was, like the kitchen, disconcerting. It was up a flight of worn stone stairs and had until very recently been used to store barley. Yet it was spacious and well lit by several large windows and had a closed-off fireplace from which hung a stovepipe. Through a small alcove there was an open balcony from which a large flooring stone had been removed. This was our bathroom, open to the elements, overlooking the back of the huge barn and three flights up due to the slope of the land. While the opening from the missing stone was too small to fall through, it was big enough to give the impression that it was a possibility. There was a definite impression of altitude and vertigo, not to mention complete visibility and the need to forego any shyness.

We borrowed brooms, swept up as well as we could, and brought up our bedding and luggage. The farmer's wife insisted on loaning us an additional cornhusk mattress, a rickety table with two old chairs and some wooden boxes to sit on, a rusty two-burner wood stove (which luckily fitted the stovepipe), a few plates, glasses, and forks. One apparently was assumed to carry the locally ubiquitous multipurpose and seldom-washed pocketknife. Not wanting to appear demanding, we bought some knives in the village. We placed all three mattresses in a corner, all of us sleeping together in order to share the blankets.

The stovepipe determined the stove location and the table and chairs were placed near the stove, where they could be used for interim storage and food preparation. Despite our cleaning efforts, we still had rats rustling around at night, I was told (I never heard them in my sound sleep), and therefore we stored what little food we had not eaten in a box hung from a convenient hook in the ceiling. For the older ones, sleeping was difficult and fitful. Arrangements for washing up were more often than not quite awkward and involved, especially since we had to bring the water up from the pump by the dishpan full. It then had to be heated if we wanted warm water. It was, of course, dumped three stories down through the toilet with a satisfying splash.

For the approximate two weeks of our stay, the days and evenings were long. Every day, after housekeeping chores, some of us went into the village for basics like bread and, more importantly, information. However, we bought most of our food from the farm: eggs, butter, milk, fresh vegetables and an occasional chicken. With nothing to do during the day we volunteered to help with the haying. This activity differed from what I was accustomed to in that the hay was barely cured and was pitchforked green and sometimes even wet into the loft, where large quantities of salt were added to eliminate spontaneous combustion. We also helped in the hand-churning of the butter every other day. The reward for helping was the afternoon *gouté*, a filling high tea type of snack similar to the one we had enjoyed when we first arrived.

Evenings, however, were a trial with little to combat the boredom and only one weak light bulb hanging from the ceiling in the center of the room. There was no radio and nothing to read other than an occasional old newspaper. By dark we were all in bed. We did, nevertheless, appreciate that we were indeed well off. Pierre quite regularly went to the village because he did not particularly enjoy physical labor and made the best of the excuse that he went primarily to seek information. It turned out that he was very competent in that, and one day on his return from Le Puy, where he had gone on a borrowed bike, he excitedly announced, 'We're going home! I've found some gas. All we have to do is go pick it up.'

It seemed that restrictions on travel that had been in effect were being lifted, that an armistice had either been signed or was about to be signed, and that we had to have a rather large amount of cash for the gas he had located. The cash we managed (although it left us without much reserve), but the real problem was how to get the gas and the car in the same place; the Renault was on empty.

Again the farmer's wife came to the rescue, selling us four bottles of home-brewed *eau-de-vie* which, with what little gas remained in the car, got it sputtering and without much power to the gasoline source, which, luckily, was not up any steep hills. With the tank and our two cans full, we returned to the farm, loaded everything up, and early the next morning (after thanking the farmer's wife warmly and expressing the hope that her husband would soon be back from the army) we left. We made the return trip in one day, encountering little traffic and only the battered and burned out wrecks that had occurred on the way out.

We drove up the village street triumphantly honking the horn and discovered that not only were we the last of those who had left to have returned, but that we needn't have left at all. Nothing had happened, Conliège was in the Non-Occupied Zone. Still, it was wonderful to be back!

July and early August were very busy for us. First we made contact with our parents in the US, who made several ship reservations for us out of Lisbon and forwarded money for both us and grandmother which we were able to pick up relatively safely and easily in Geneva. Since grandmother insisted on staying in France, we did our best to help her get ready for the winter and the unknown, unfinished war.

With the assistance of the farmers I had regularly helped with haying in previous summers, we hauled and cut several cords of wood; located and transported huge burlap bags of sawdust (which burned slowly in the stoves in lieu of coal, as we had discovered the past winter); went up to the plateau with hand carts to collect all the pine cones we could find; cut endless amounts of vineyard trimmings into kindling; made sauerkraut; dug two of the large boxwood-bordered lawn squares of the formal garden into future vegetable garden plots; built two more rabbit hutches; and laid in all the canned goods, sugar, and cooking oil we could locate. Finally, before mid-August, the time for departure had arrived. The time was guesstimated by how long it would take to reach Lisbon, all the more unsubstantiated since we were not certain what crossing the frontier into Spain would involve.

Our departure was undoubtedly more of an emotional strain on our grandmother than on us. While we were concerned about leaving her alone and nervous about whatever unknowns we might encounter, we had the optimism of youth and rather enjoyed the whole idea of this adventure. We left confidently on a beautiful, sunny market day for Lons, taking advantage of the little trolley that came down from Saint-Claude. We then took the train from Lons to Avignon. We each carried a small suitcase, having decided that suitcases better suited two young vacationers on their way to visit Spain than the rucksacks that many refugees seemed to carry. We also had a musette bag for food that contained mainly bread and cheese. I, who until then had shunned cheese as an inedible thing, would have to learn to like it; it was that or go hungry. We had originally planned to stay in Avignon, but the local train to Perpignan was immediately available and we jumped on board, reaching our destination early that evening. I remember the meal of eggplant, tomatoes, and garlic swimming in much strong olive oil we received in a small local restaurant. Perhaps I remember it because I had not eaten the bread and cheese we had with us and I was starving.

The next day we took a smaller 'milk run' local to the frontier town of Cerbère. It was crowded with an odd mix of passengers: locals getting on and off at every stop, gossiping in their strong southern French accents and intonations or arguing heatedly that if the vineyard owners did not kill a pig for the help, they could certainly expect to pick the grapes all by themselves (*s'ils ne le tuent pas le cochon, ils peuvent bien se les cueillir les raisins*); a few non-locals who were obviously French by their different accents, clothing, mannerisms and their rather restrained conversation limited to the members of their own group; and finally a group who were neither local nor French, individuals of all ages who sat in strained, tired silence.

We all got off as it was the end of the line (the rail gauge in Spain was wider than in France); the locals quickly and certain of their destinations, but the rest of us more slowly and hesitantly. We were among the last, and as we approached the entrance to the customs area we encountered some of our fellow non-local French passengers (who had preceded us) coming out, complaining despondently and indignantly among themselves that the frontier was closed.

While this was disconcerting for us, the stress and worry of the non-French travelers, whose comprehension of that announcement was uncertain, was quite manifest. Not trusting hearsay, we went into the customs area, received the same news from the only person there, but with the additional bit of information that things would be operating the next day with 'damned visitors' present. Until now we travelers had scarcely acknowledged each other's existence, much less talked to one another, so we were somewhat taken aback on our way out when one of the non-French travelers asked in very halting, heavily-accented French what had been said. When we had finally succeeded in making ourselves understood, he shook his head sadly saying, 'police allemande' and left with two others.

A short stroll through Cerbère convinced us there was no place to spend the night, so we boarded the same train and went back one stop to Banyuls-sur-Mer, more of a resort town, where we found a room. The next morning we returned to Cerbère and found the border facilities occupied by Germans, some in uniform and some civilians, with *feldgrau* vehicles parked in front. They were very much in charge and openly directed the French personnel. This, of course, was a direct contravention of the independence of the Non-Occupied Zone that, by the terms of the armistice, was to remain under French control. We were again told the border would be closed 'until later'. While we had no real reason to be concerned about getting through, since we had valid passports, the shock of finding Germans obviously in control of what was supposed to be the Non-Occupied Zone made us uneasy.

We decided to examine any possible alternatives for crossing into Spain. This was without a doubt motivated by a mix on the one hand of youthful, adventurous bravado (for we had, I am sure, no intention of trying any alternative methods of crossing unless it should become absolutely necessary for unforeseeable reasons) and primarily, on the other hand, of the necessity to kill some time. We checked the suitcases and strolled around, noticing very soon that others seemed to be doing the same thing. Whether they were looking for alternative exits or just killing time was hard to determine, though some of the non-French travelers seemed more intent and went further afield in their ramblings.

It was immediately obvious that crossing the mountains in the immediate vicinity was not promising; there was very little vegetation for cover which would necessitate a night crossing with no knowledge of the terrain or of the presence of any guards, nor even of where the frontier was located. The seashore appeared completely unguarded and, at first glance, seemed more promising. We walked along the beach till we came to the border, which was marked by a very casual fence that went out a short distance into the water. While it could have been possible to swim or wade around it, or even climb over it, it might have meant discarding luggage and it would have been difficult to keep money, papers, and clothing dry. While the area was apparently unguarded at the time, it was sure to be watched for night-time attempts to cross the border. Whatever few boats were on the beach were obviously not simple, two-man operations to launch and they were missing oars. There still remained the unknowns of the Spanish coast and Port Bou from where the train to Barcelona left.

We returned to the station and sipped a drink from the buffet while waiting for the train to return us to our room in Banyuls. We watched the operation of the border and customs which were finally functioning. It appeared that there were no particular difficulties or obstacles for the few who were being processed then.

The next morning, having decided the night before to go ahead with crossing into Spain, we proceeded as we had planned with the formalities. We crossed the station square where *feldgrau* army vehicles were parked, bought our tickets to Port Bou and entered the customs area where there were not only uniformed officials but also several men in leather coats stationed near the exits. Pierre went first while I remained behind for follow-up if something untoward happened to him. Based on the previous day's observations, we thought we could select a line leading to the two or three officials examining papers, thereby choosing one who by some undefined aura seemed more accommodating.

That morning, however, everyone was formed into a single line and a French civilian directed the next eligible person to whichever official was available at the tables. We each passed through different officials, both very proper and polite and dressed in uniforms that were foreign to us. They used very pronounced German-accented French, and neither of us had any problems with the interview, although as we compared notes afterwards we were concerned because each had given a different place as our destination in Spain. We rationalized hopefully that Valencia and Barcelona were at least plausible vacation areas neither too far from one another nor sufficiently far south to arouse suspicions of an escape attempt to Africa, and besides we had been processed by different personnel.

We immediately boarded the train to Port Bou, which did not leave for almost an hour as we waited for the other passengers to get through the formalities. The short ride to Spain led to another frontier formality, no difficulties, and another long wait for the train to Barcelona. During that wait, charged with relief, tension and anticipation, we decided not to destroy Pierre's French passport because the station area was so small that it would be too risky. Instead we occupied some of the time changing some francs for pesetas. These were worn, dirty, and of very limited denominations, and we quickly discovered that change was not often given in coin but usually with postage stamps, equally worn, wrinkled and greasy. I don't remember ever handling a coin while in Spain. Knowing no Spanish, we were undoubtedly short-changed often. While Cerbère was not opulent in any way, it almost seemed so in comparison to Port Bou, where everything was dirty and run down. We had finished the last of our bread and cheese by the time the train pulled out for Barcelona, for by then I was able to eat a nibble of cheese with each bite of bread with a degree of enthusiasm.

We arrived in Barcelona in the early afternoon and, although the train for Madrid did not leave for several hours, we stayed in the station after buying our tickets rather than adventuring out to be tourists. We were somewhat taken aback by the large number of police patrolling in pairs in their conspicuous black, tri-cornered leather hats. Perhaps it was their singular presence that led us to the untimely decision that now was the time to get rid of Pierre's

French passport. We took turns tearing it up in the *retretes* (the public privies) some of which were mere holes in the floor with two small steps on which to balance. The inside pages bearing the visas were relatively easy to tear into very small pieces, but the cover was very tough and took much energy and effort to tear even into semi-conspicuous segments. All these bits of paper were evenly distributed into all the available *retretes* and repeatedly flushed in those where that facility existed. The frequency of our trips to the *retretes*, not to mention our furtively nonchalant approach to the whole operation, should have been enough to have caught the attention of the ubiquitous *Guardia Civil*. We left for Madrid quite satisfied with ourselves and quite optimistic.

It was a long trip for the train seldom seemed to go much above an exhaustingly slow clickety-clack. It was dark when the train pulled into a large, dimly lit station (possibly Zaragoza). We were riding in old railroad cars where the compartment comprised the whole width of the carriage with doors that opened out on each side. Famished, we opened the compartment door nearest the station from which we were separated by an adjoining track. We left the carriage door open and crossed the adjoining track and purchased some unknown food package. As we were waiting for our change, we heard a whistle and saw our train starting to move. We ran across the tracks and managed to get on the running board of a car (luckily it was ours) and thanks to the waving of one of the other occupants found our compartment. We ate the miserable, expensive pastry we had purchased and suffered from thirst until we finally reached Madrid late at night.

We were in the station buffet finishing a drink after having checked our luggage when two *Guardia Civil* came by checking everyone's papers. It seemed to be a very cursory examination. There was no trouble with my French passport. They looked only at the information on the page containing the photo, but the fact that the same name also appeared on a US passport seemed to arouse their curiosity. They looked at the pages for visas and apparently noticed the lack of a French one. They walked us to the nearest police station, and after much discussion by the personnel there, we were taken by car to a large facility where someone who spoke a little French asked us where we had crossed and why we were in Spain. We told him we crossed at Cerbère/Port Bou and that we were on vacation. We insisted that we had gone through normally, describing all the formalities and asking them to get in touch with the American consul. In the end we were assured that the consulate would be notified of our predicament and would no doubt send someone around 'as usual', but that Pierre would have to remain a prisoner until the matter of his 'illegal entry' was resolved. At our request, I was allowed to stay with him, and together we were escorted to a large holding cell where others were already sleeping, dozing or just sitting. There was no talking and the inmates seemed to be both Spanish and non-Spanish.

The holding cell was not too crowded, but as might be expected it was very dirty. The few cots with very soiled, thin pads as mattresses were occupied. There was trash on the floor and odiferous *retretes* in one corner. We spent an uncomfortable remainder of the night, worried, silent and dozing while seated on the floor until we were served bread and something that might pass for weak coffee for breakfast.

Our acceptance of the stated certainty that the American Embassy would resolve everything weakened as the day went by, and we took every opportunity to try to find out from the guards when the embassy official normally came. We then tried to ascertain if he had indeed been notified of our existence and problem.

We spent the second night in a restless, pessimistic struggle between our imaginations and a growing and oppressive despondency. It was only several anguishing hours after the morning bread and *ersatz* coffee had been consumed that an American representing the embassy finally appeared, questioned us about our lives in America, and seemed reassuringly confident that he could see no reason why we should be held since our papers were, in fact, in order for travel in Spain. He felt it could be taken care of quite expeditiously.

Our spirits soared. He told us he would use his influence, but it was said in such a way that it was obvious that some transaction on his part would be undertaken to dispose the proper authorities to expedite matters. We spent what seemed an interminable time waiting anxiously for some word. He sent word just after our early dinner of soup and bread to tell us all was well and that the paperwork for our release was being finished; however, we weren't finally signed out of the Miranda prison until early the next morning after yet another, albeit more relaxed and optimistic, night of incarceration. We received all our belongings intact and gave a Spanish official a tip of a few dollars as the American had suggested. He in turn then gave us an official paper certifying that we were in order.

We took a cab to the station, where we retrieved our luggage, bought tickets for Lisbon, ate an unpleasant meal, cleaned up as well as we could in the somewhat cleaner and more modern public washroom and joined the large crowd getting on the train. We successfully managed to get one seat. We took turns standing in the corridor for the slow, endless trip to Elvas at the Portuguese border. I fell asleep several times standing in the corridor.

The border crossing was a mere formality; I don't remember that we even had to detrain. Then as the train moved out, immediately and magically the whole ambience aboard changed. Many passengers had gotten off, making a seat available to us and now there was loud talking, laughter, friendly exchanges of food and drink, among both foreign and Portuguese travelers. One Portuguese offered us wine, showing us how to drink from a skin pouch with the spout held away from the mouth. The trick, which to everyone's amusement I never mastered, was to squeeze the pouch and have the flow of liquid go straight down your gullet with no swallowing involved. No such interaction had ever occurred as we traveled through defeated France or Franco's Spain.

Immediately upon our arrival in Lisbon we looked up the address of American Export Lines and changed money (including change for those wonderfully solid escudos which clinked satisfyingly in our pockets). Mid-morning found us at the Lines' office inquiring about the reservations our parents had made. Were in luck: *Excalibur* had docked just recently and we could have a cabin when it sailed within the next two days. Elated, we found a hotel, cleaned up, ate and slept. The next day we wandered around Lisbon and even took a train to Estoril, where we enjoyed a walk on the beach.

The next afternoon we boarded *Excalibur*. It was a rather large freighter with quite extensive passenger accommodation, far more than the passenger freighters of today. The midship section was devoted entirely to passenger service and included a dining room, a library, a promenade deck, shuffle board, deck tennis and ping-pong. Like on regular passenger liners, bouillon was served mid-morning and tea in the afternoon. Admittedly, the service was not as polished as on the French Line but much better from our point of view: there was cold cereal, milk, soft drinks, hamburgers and even ICE CREAM! It was a real treat. The head steward, who seemed to be everywhere, had that reassuringly strong Brooklyn accent that epitomized the overall informality and friendliness of the ship's operation.

We had an outside cabin that we shared with two French boys whose parents and sister were in another cabin and who were going to contact friends in New York. Pierre, as the oldest in the group, took responsibility for the cabin and claimed the lower berth, so I had the top one without the usual bickering between us for that privilege. The week-long trip was a pleasure; no nervous, stressful situations, food readily and plentifully available, other people our age with whom to play deck tennis, ping-pong, and talk, and the ego-enhancing position of being one of the few persons on board familiar with the US who were perfectly bilingual. Even the fact that huge US flags had been painted on the sides of the ship with large searchlights mounted outboard to illuminate them implied safety rather than potential danger.

We docked in New Jersey and were met by our parents, who had to wait quite some time for us to disembark because Pierre had opted to wait to go through immigration with me rather than go ahead of the non-citizens, which his US passport entitled him to do. As a result, he was given a serious lecture about why he should have gone ahead of all the foreigners by the immigration personnel, who were not only unconcerned about a family relationship, but never noticed that his passport bore no visas. The family reunion was, as expected, emotional and followed by an excellent meal at our Tante Margot's apartment. The next day we were back home in Massachusetts.

The next two and a half years I spent in school. I did not graduate from Deerfield Academy in June of 1941, where I was a 'day-boy' commuting the twenty-eight miles each day, because the school principal convinced my disbelieving mother that I was too young and immature to enter college. He was absolutely right, and thus Pearl Harbor found me still in school struggling with a physics course that I loathed.

The summers of '41 and '42 I spent on an old New England farm, haying, milking cows, pumping water, chopping wood and doing many other miscellaneous chores. I earned seven dollars a week plus board and room and enjoyed the experience immensely, especially as it was not all work and no play. There was square dancing every Friday night with the daughter of the household at the local Grange Hall. In fact, I also spent several spring vacations helping with the sugaring.

In the fall of '43 I entered Harvard. I waited on tables at Dunster House having to trudge there early in the morning from Gray's Hall in the Yard. The dining in those days consisted of a full menu with choice of entrées, and it was operated like a regular first class restaurant. I rather enjoyed the work, although for some unknown reason (perhaps because I, too, spoke French) I had some very wealthy South American students who regularly sat at my tables. It may also just have been that the tables were in a corner near windows. Unfortunately, they liked to dine late and would come in just before the dining room closed. Weekdays were not too bad, but on weekends they came with their dates and kept ordering extras and lingered over coffee. Yet what I minded most of all was their ordering of grapefruit, which the waiter had to prepare individually and was time consuming. It also complicated serving the other tables. I would get home late, which did not help my study habits.

I wasted much of the early part of that freshman year with my roommate, who was an admirer of Max Ernst, not doing much serious studying and cutting classes with immature abandon. I had tried to enlist in the Navy, but not being a citizen I could not. I had also toyed with the idea of joining the Free French where, according to a colleague of my father, I could have gotten a second lieutenant's commission. I wisely chose not to. I just waited for my draft notice.

CHAPTER 2

When I finally received my draft notice I was delighted and relieved. I knew I had not accomplished much in the first half of the year, having goofed off with my eccentric and wild roommate, and no real improvement was likely in what remained of the second semester. I had played the role of the immature freshman away from home for the first time to perfection, unconcerned about organizing my time between my classes, waiting on tables and studying. The possibility of even getting acceptable 'gentlemanly C's' seemed rather remote and 'D's' appeared probable. After all, I had already made the Dean's List, not the meritorious one, but the one warning me of a dangerously unsatisfactory attendance record. I suppose my immature enthusiasm for going off to war may in some respects have been a subconscious acceptance in part of an apparent God-given escape from an unhappy situation; more likely I was caught up in the emotional enthusiasm of the day. I immediately went to the college authorities to notify them of my departure and went home for a week before my induction date.

Leaving home for the war was not the traumatic experience that I had read about or expected from my close, controlling family. I had had a very protective childhood with few playmates other than my brother, in part due to my professor parents, whose French chauvinism reinforced and nurtured the natural division between town and gown, and who brought us up in accordance with current French bourgeois standards in complete contradiction to informal American ways, even to the point of sending me to my first several sessions at dance school in short pants. I thankfully then got my first long pants suit; it had even come with two pairs of pants, but the impact of being so out of the norm had already had some effect.

We spoke French at home all the time, and 'Jean, *parle français*' was a constant refrain. Being called home in French, whether for meals or from play, was another constant that I considered an indignity in my childhood. My father (whose favorite I probably was) for the most part believed that children should be seen and not heard. He had, in fact, no relationship with his children and no objective for them other than good scholarship. He and mother scarcely got along – no fights, just a bare tolerance of one another. Mother was a very controlling and extremely sentimental woman, spoiled by her father, but inwardly very tough.

All of this must have contributed to the weak development of my self-confidence, a considerable timidity on my part in interactions outside the family and an astounding lack of knowledge of the real world around me. I was just beginning to branch out by the time I was called up. I am sure there was a resulting anticipatory guilt that perhaps I was insensitive to my parents' feelings, but my youthful optimism and excitement made it difficult for me to appear duly stricken in a situation I expected to be rather emotional. Yet other than admonitions to be sure to write, I don't remember any signifi-cant parental expressions of sentiment, much less emotional scenes, as we waited for the train. Perhaps it was that they had already gone through the same thing with my brother less than six months before and, after all, he was still in training and due home on leave soon. So it was that we parted with a mutually rather casual wave (though hiding a rather worried expectancy on my part) as the train pulled out.

Several hours later I was in a whole new world, whose novelty and confusion was such that I find I remember almost nothing of the details of my first days in the Army. I vaguely remember a sort of clamorous registration, carrying papers from one place to another, receiving shots (which I disliked), but beyond that very few personal memories. I know, according to my discharge papers, that I was inducted and sworn in on 9 June 1943 at Fort Devens, MA, amid considerable confusion and yells of 'You'll be sorry' as we tramped from one building to another, but aside from being 'volunteered' for KP, that first muddled night, I remember almost nothing.

I do have a clear memory of being told to clean the swill box during KP duty. The smell made me nearly sick to my stomach, and I left it as I had found it and walked away from the mess hall without permission long before KP duties were over. Considering my obedient compliance to direction at home, this was probably a move of desperation.

I do not remember being assigned to a barracks, to a bed, being issued clothing, fed, or falling out for formations, nor even for how long I remained at Fort Devens. I feel it was not very long for I am quite uncertain whether we were in uniform or still in our civilian clothes when I boarded a troop train one morning to go to a basic training destination. I do remember still carrying the overnight bags we had brought from home and not struggling with any duffel bags. However, we all already felt ourselves sufficiently experienced to call out 'You'll be sorry' to incoming newcomers while still being impressed by staff personnel wearing the ubiquitous Good Conduct ribbon.

It was a long trip from Fort Devens to Camp Croft, SC. Not only had we no idea of our destination, but the old day coaches which we occupied to their full capacity offered little comfort for that long journey. The seats were arranged so that four persons faced one another with very limited legroom. The closeness was uncomfortable enough during the day with our knees constantly bumping, but it was even more trying at night, as we tried to position ourselves to get some sleep. The journey lasted two long days and a night, with occasional long stops in the middle of nowhere for other traffic to move through. Three times a day we were 'escorted' to a former mail car that had been converted into a kitchen where we were served hot meals on paper plates (this was before they were coated with plastic) which we balanced as best we could along with paper cups, napkins, and silverware as we made our unsteady way through the swaying cars back to our seats where we ate the stew or 'Italian' pasta on our laps as quickly as possible before the plates became sodden and leaked.

Where to balance our cups while we ate was another of the many frustrations. Of course there was no air conditioning, and the soot from the steam engines (which blew in through the open windows and covered everything) made our mashed potatoes appear very heavily peppered. After meals we had to police the area (a new term added to my vocabulary) taking plates to a trash can and silverware to a large tub of water in which they were presumably washed.

Bathroom facilities were limited to the rest rooms at each end of the car, and they were virtually inaccessible most of the time. But it was a wonderful adventure for the immature kid I was. For the most part there was very little griping, except when the drinking water containers at the ends of each car were empty and the combination of sooty hot air and the radiation from a hot southern sun made things far from comfortable. The escort personnel finally had someone refill them periodically before morning on the second day (but without ice).

We had been told to take the next available seat as we came to it on boarding and I was lucky. My seatmates included two Czechs who spoke a strongly accented English and a prep school teacher, all of them older than I by at least some ten years. All three had had the foresight to bring a book, one had a cribbage board and another a miniature chess set whose pieces fitted into holes to keep them in place. I learned to play cribbage and a little chess, and more importantly to always have some means of killing time. They knew very little more than I about army life, but were cheerful and optimistic individuals of the more mature, well-educated type of person with whom I was most familiar and comfortable.

Arrival at Camp Croft late the second day was methodical and organized. We were 'marched' directly from the siding where the train had stopped in the camp to the front of the barracks, where we were counted off and led inside to take the next available bed. Each bed had the necessary linen and a towel. We were then taught how to make beds with hospital corners and taut sheets, which were briefly inspected by a loud, authoritative corporal who informed us that henceforth a quarter should bounce when dropped on the sheets at inspection. This, of course, never happened.

We were then led to the mess hall, given instructions while we ate a late meal about not short-stopping food when passing it and, finally, after a brief visit by some officer who gave us a welcoming speech for which we had all been called to attention (a minor thrill this first time), we were marched back to barracks and reminded that tomorrow started early. Most of us managed a most welcome shower before collapsing into bed at Taps.

The next few days we were occupied receiving more shots, being issued many items of clothing (a set of suntans [sic], a pair of boots, two sets of fatigues, underwear and towels) as well as a variety of equipment (canteen, mess kit, leggings, belt, pack, helmet and helmet liner, a rifle and an entrenching tool). In personal matters our sergeant was helpful, advising us to walk through puddles with our new boots and to keep them on till dry so that they would be broken in to the shape of our feet more quickly, but when dealing with anything pertaining to military training, such concern seemed to disappear.

So we began formally to be introduced to our new military existence in repetitive stages. Initially, just managing to shave and shower in the morning rush and to be ready was a quite nerve-wracking experience, but very quickly became normal. Overall, it was a relatively painless adjustment, the focus and control being so completely in the trainers' favor, and the trainees' desire to belong and do well quickly, molded us into a motivated, if clumsy, platoon. As one of the few who had never seen or handled a rifle before, I had difficulty at first with the disassembly and reassembly of the M–1 and particularly its cleaning: this was a minor problem which was resolved with the help of a drafted state trooper who provided very helpful tips on the best way to get and keep it clean.

I must admit that I rather enjoyed those three months of basic training, even though (or perhaps primarily because) everything was so completely new and different from anything I had ever experienced. This new exposure to life in general and its American realities was unexpected, overwhelming, fascinating and so unknown as to require a complete readjustment of my view of things. I knew normal swear words, and even knew of the word 'shit' (as excrement, not as an expletive). Hard as it is to believe now, I had never heard the word 'fuck' or 'motherfucker'. That I still remember the corporal's first awakening call of 'OK you motherfuckers! Drop your cocks and grab your socks. Let's go!' is an indication of the impression it must have made on me.

Also, the men in the platoon I was with were a totally foreign mix for me. They comprised Boston North End Italians (one of whom, judging from his silk shirt, shoes, clothes, jewelry – which he sorrowfully packed to ship home – along with his constant complaining about everything, led many of us to assume Mafia associations), a few odd men from Tennessee we sort of considered bumpkins, probably because of their new-to-us accent (one of whom managed to get an erection during our first short-arm inspection, creating a wild hubbub of reaction even from the medical officer), some refined Southerners from North Carolina (who gave me my first acquaintance with the theory of the 'fairness' of racism during some of the bull sessions we had), and my foreign traveling companions on the way down with whom I still seemed to have the most in common.

Like so many other trainees, we survived the routine basic training quite easily in spite of the usual uproar of preparation for Saturday inspection, complicated several times by the water from the floor washing of the second story leaking onto our spotless, completed downstairs effort; in spite of the periodic KP, where on one occasion, when spare ribs had been served, the hot water heater provided only tepid water and it was after 2 a.m. and three washings (the last with stove-heated water) before the dishes, pots and pans met the Mess Sergeant's approval and he still kept us lining up the plates so that, looking down the mess hall, the place settings were in a straight line down all the tables; in spite of the bitter sense of unfairness in one of the weapons inspections when I once was docked for having sand on my rifle butt from putting it down on commands of parade rest and attention just as the inspection started; in spite of the mind deadening dry run rifle target practice in the July South Carolina heat; in spite of passing out once from that heat while standing in formation; in spite of walking naked except for raincoats in the summer heat on our way to whatever purpose was served by our only swimming break; in spite of the useless and very boring walking around for long hours in the night in the middle of a fenced and guarded military camp doing guard duty. The fifteen cent pitcher of 3.2% beer in the camp 'beer garden' in the evening with its bull sessions made up for any disagreeable moments during the day, particularly the limited water in our canteens during exercises in the July and August heat, presumably rationed to get us ready for duty in North Africa, which, rumor had it, was to be our destination. There were changes in the group as some were assigned to other units and schools. Like everything else, it was a completely new experience.

In the midst of these training activities two events occurred. One day, with no advance warning, I was gratefully called off the dry run firing range along with several others. We were driven by truck to Spartanburg, where we were all sworn in as citizens. I was, of course, delighted, but several others protested, among them my two Czech friends, who were very willing to serve in the US Army, but wanted to retain their native citizenship. They disappeared soon after.

I was called away a second time and told to report to an office near headquarters. There I was interviewed by a Major (the highest rank I had ever encountered) who questioned me about my French, all in English, and talked about some sort of special service. No explanation or hint of what that special service might entail, but if I was interested would I complete the application he was giving me and mail it in. Seeing no particular reason for not complying, I took it, saluted and left.

I spent the next several weeks completing the sixteen pages of questions, writing home to get information from my parents and cursing the nonsense of the entire interview. In complete innocence, I answered every question fully, even those concerning family in France whom I scarcely knew.

At the end of basic training I requested and obtained a transfer to the paratroops. I had immaturely fallen in love with the glamour of jump boots (perhaps in rejection of the old-fashioned canvas leggings we had been issued), my sole motivation for such a move. Armed with orders and carrying my duffel bag, I reported to Fort Benning, where I was put on temporary duty with a small group pending the start of a formal training session. After about a week of pushups, running and KP, I was called into the company office, told to pack my things, return to pick up orders, and be ready to leave.

It was not until I was at the station waiting for the train that I opened the envelope and discovered my destination was Washington, D.C. I left without having obtained those longed-for paratrooper boots, and was again to face an unknown situation after the familiarity and 'normalcy' of basic training.

On arrival in Washington on an early September morning, I took a taxi to the E Street address on the orders. It was a large, multi-story, whitish building in a rather shabby neighborhood (at least in comparison to the official buildings I had driven by). I entered somewhat confused, my duffel bag in hand. The guard had me wait a short time in the corridor before I was escorted, without my bag, to a room on an upper floor where another (to me, pointless and uninformative) interview took place, but this time conducted in French by someone who had a good command of the language but was patently not native though very fluent. I don't remember any questions concerning my willingness to participate in clandestine operations, but I must have satisfied all his requirements for he disappeared for a while and, on his return, gave me some papers to sign, mentioned something about training to occur somewhere, welcomed me aboard OSS, and stressed that I was not to mention the word OSS or what I was doing to anyone. Since I was not too certain what OSS stood for and it had never been more than vaguely explained to me what I might be going to do, and since I was too dumb or timid to inquire, the admonition now appears as superfluous as when it was uttered.

More immediately interesting was that I was given a chit of some kind and a two-week pass. On my return I was told to be in front of the Willard Hotel at twelve fifteen and 'board the army truck' when it stopped. No other information or details were provided or requested. Yet the sense of mystery these instructions should have implied was superseded by my delight at the forthcoming pass arrangement, and all in all I felt a keen sense of anticipation about going home and was very self-satisfied. I returned to the station and, finding I had several hours to kill, checked my bag and went for a stroll. Fresh from basic training, I dutifully saluted each of the multitude of officers I met until some kindly Lt. Colonel stopped me to say, 'Son, you don't have to salute on the street here.' Things were certainly looking up!

During my time at home I learned that my brother Pierre had been there just the previous week and that he had announced that it looked like he was to be stationed in the Washington area. Mother was delighted when I mentioned that it seemed I, too, might be stationed there (never mentioning the forbidden word OSS). She already had us working together. It never entered my mind that perhaps she knew more than I, and as I afterward discovered, she didn't. I returned to Washington certain that mother's hope that we brothers could probably get together sometime was more than improbable, he being in the Air Corps and I in the Army.

At twelve sharp I stood anxiously in the lobby of the Willard tensely awaiting the mysterious truck. I noticed other persons in the lobby, some in uniform and others in civilian clothing, who also seemed to be waiting and viewing the street, but I thought little of it, being too immersed in my own nervous expectation. When an army truck appeared and stopped at the appointed time, to my astonishment a good portion of the people in the lobby moved out to the street. The driver collected our chits and we climbed aboard. I was further surprised to see that many of the civilians and military knew each other, and while they indulged in chatting about their weekends and shop talk, I sat mutely not knowing my destination or what was going on. I did suspect that there could be very little of a truly clandestine nature in this regularly scheduled pickup; it was my first introduction to the cynical actuality of the many over-employed security theories with which we were initially burdened.

After about an hour's ride we turned off onto a little dirt road and ended up in what I later learned was Area C, located near Quantico and Fort Belvoir, MD. It had been a Girl Scout camp and relatively little had been done to equip it for its present usage other than the addition of several larger buildings that were used as classrooms and a mess hall. The sleeping quarters I was assigned to were still the same rustic structures with only screening on the windows and four to six cots. The common bath facilities, however, had been improved and expanded, the food was good, the routine simple, the discipline relaxed and the training varied and quite fascinating. Overall, I enjoyed the three months spent there. Additionally, almost every weekend we were off and in possession of a pass with free transportation to and from Washington. My current girlfriend was in training with the Waves in New York and I experienced the long, deadening return ride in the very late night/early morning (very often having to stand all the way) as frequently as my private's pay would allow.

On arrival, the returnees had drifted off, leaving a small group of us to be escorted to a classroom where we were briefed. We were to learn what was necessary for clandestine operations (not well defined but clearly rather specific), we would be using first names only to assure anonymity, and everything was to be on an informal basis (no ranks). When several of us pointed out that our names were stenciled on our duffel bags, we were told to keep them in the bottom of our foot lockers which were out of bounds to everyone. After suggesting we change into our fatigues before we reported back in twenty-five minutes, we were escorted to our cabins. I was dropped off alone in front of one, found an unoccupied/unmade bed, changed, and dutifully put my stuff away in the 'safe foot locker' and reported back to the room to receive more briefings, which finally made clearer in a general way the clandestine objectives for which we were to be trained.

As I stepped out of the training room door, I literally bumped into my brother. Surprisingly, we both managed a non-committal 'excuse me' and shortly after went through the charade of a formal introduction by a college friend of his whom I also knew. We both took the same training but in different groups in different sequence, so that while we saw little of each other in training we did manage to spend considerable time together, especially since it turned out we had been assigned the same cabin.

In retrospect, the training was somewhat all purpose, general, a sampling, at best the equivalent of a college survey course. We were introduced to many subjects but developed real expertise in none. This was probably due, of course, to the fact that there were no specific assignments or missions to prepare for. Nevertheless, as a basic catch-all preparation it did serve its purpose, so that every day we were presented with a varied assortment of subjects in two- to four-hour sessions. With the exception of learning Morse code, which required more involvement and time, I never felt any subject presented to be overwhelming or lacking in interest. It was all so different, unfamiliar, and tantalizingly full of prospects.

There was much emphasis on weapons training, handling (firing, cleaning, and disassembling) a large variety of pistols, revolvers, and automatics of many calibers and nationalities. We fired these weapons over courses through the woods where targets would pop up as you ran the course, and learned to shoot from a crouch without really taking aim. Strangely, I found that I, who had barely made Marksman in basic training when doing my best carefully to aim and, more carefully, to squeeze off the shots, could be more effective and accurate with this approach. A Major Fairburn of the Shanghai police taught us elements of hand-to-hand fighting and how to use the Fairburn knife with its well-balanced double-edged blade and introduced us to the kosh (a solid steel ball attached to a strong spring in three segments which slid over one another into a hollow metal handle and very forcefully extended some three feet when swung or directed at a target).

Also involved were many long sessions of demolition training, dealing with black powder, TNT, plastics, primacord and even flour, as well as booby trapping devices and time delay blasting caps (small color-coded tubes which when crushed would detonate a charge after a specified delay with some degree of accuracy and reliability), but here again the entire emphasis was on the handling of explosives with very little presentation of their use and placement for effective or specific purposes. In fact, a fellow trainee had to contact London when operational to get help on where to place a second set of charges on a bridge he was trying to blow up. We all felt a certain nervousness initially, as much for our own novice handling and per-haps even more for that of our classmates as we learned to crimp fuse to blasting caps and light them or set up booby traps with pressure release devices, but we quickly gained confidence as we realized that we all did indeed know what we were doing.

All this activity was interspersed with map reading and making simple maps, and we sometimes used maps made by previous classes. In one instance we ended up having to wade in some thoroughly misplaced swamp. We also learned some basic guerrilla tactics as well as regular physical exercise every morning.

All the paramilitary-type training culminated in two separate night exercises. The first involved half the group being assigned to the defense of a house and the rest playing the role of attackers. My memory of it, as one of the defenders, was of a confused fiasco, waiting in the dark away from the house to give the alert and help in any counter-attack but with no pre-arranged signals, organization, or planning.

The second exercise involved 'destroying' a small bridge with the same division of roles. As one of the attack group, I volunteered to be one of the party who came down the stream behind and under a floating log and some branches and successfully managed to steer the contraption to where we could effectively place the charges of 'explosives' while the rest created a diversionary attack. While the success was wonderfully gratifying, I mostly remember how cold I was during and immediately after that long immersion for it was mid-November.

The training for the more clandestine operations was also covered, but very scantily. We had one week where we were supposed to hide our true identity from everyone else by pretending to be someone other than ourselves; I put on what I suspect was more a parody of a British accent. While it was fun, it proved nothing and was never critiqued. The whole complex and important subject of clandestine communication was treated as a question of radio transmission and dealt with mainly by the teaching of Morse code, although there was passing mention of dead drops, invisible inks, and how to 'steam' open envelopes. We were even given practice in picking locks, though we never got past the three-tumbler variety (I still have a partial set of rakes that supposedly facilitated the job).

The more critical subject, that of dealing with the making of personal contact arrangements (and simultaneously making alternative ones as backup or practicing such contacts including recognition and danger signals) were not touched upon. Indeed, the only personal contact training I received, while partially applicable, was more the opposite of making contact, consisting as it did of two brief practice sessions in Baltimore, where we tried tailing someone in the first and then losing a tail or not being spotted in the other. I must admit that those sessions did show the real difficulty of the task as no lecture or movie could get across. Nevertheless, we spent tedious hours copying Morse code, with occasional moments of triumph and satisfaction as we passed from one word-per-minute rate to the next: but then immediately the relative facility of copying at the old rate suddenly disappeared and the frustration of code coming in faster than you could handle it brought you back to the feeling that you were just starting all over again. I achieved eighteen words per minute (each word was a group of five randomly selected letters), and shortly after that, whether that was the speed required for graduation or whether some other factor was involved in the decision, I was promoted to corporal and sent to Fort Hamilton, New York, for shipment overseas. Pierre, who was now a sergeant, was again in the same group.

For several days we were able to obtain passes to go into New York off duty and saw our parents twice at Tante Margot's apartment. There was a certain solemnity and tenseness at those family gatherings over our forthcoming departure. My aunt and uncle's wonderful meals never really succeeded in overcoming the tension.

While at the Fort, there were the usual pre-shipment procedures, shots, record updating, movies, and lectures, including a booklet on how to get along with the English we were to meet, with emphasis on some of the differences between British English and American English. We were also issued gas masks, another item to account for and carry, and went through a room with tear gas, I suppose to verify that they fit and to give us confidence.

On the morning of 23 December we had a chance to make a brief call to say our passes had been cancelled with the obvious news that this implied. At dusk three days later we were loaded into a truck and driven to the ship. I believe it was called the *Christian Heugen*. It was a nondescript old thing that must have carried passengers as well as freight in its day in the Dutch East Indies service. We sailed at dawn three days after Christmas.

Our OSS group, under a master sergeant who carried all our records and was presumably in charge of the group, was quartered several decks down (I don't remember seeing any portholes) in a fairly large, dead-end area divided by an aisle on each side of which were four green metal tables seating eight persons each on attached benches. It was here that we ate, amused ourselves, and slept for what seemed a very long twelve days. The sleeping arrangements consisted of hammocks slung above and across the tables each taking up about three feet of space. It took a certain agility to get in or out of them as they swayed in unison with the roll of the ship. Every day we converted our sleeping quarters to daytime use by taking down most of the hammocks and storing them in a few left hanging, just to give us a feeling of space and the ability to stand upright outside the aisle.

Meals were provided in a single pail. Each table had a number and one of us would go to the kitchen somewhere aft, give our table number and receive a pail into which eight servings were dumped. Thus for breakfast eight dollops of oatmeal would go in first, to be followed by eight hardboiled eggs, jam then toast – or pudding for dessert would be sitting on top of the stew. This mess had to be dished out into our mess kits. Luckily, the coffee or tea came in a separate pot. The kitchen washed the pails and pots when we returned them, but the cleaning up of our mess kits had to be done by us in the latrine sinks using our own soap and towels with somewhat dubious sanitary results.

During the day we were allowed on deck and had the reassuring sight of the large convoy of which we were part. Our sorties on deck were usually short, both because it was so crowded, but mainly because it was so cold and smoking on deck was not allowed. The only place other than our quarters available for diversion was a windowless box of a structure set up near the stern, devoid of furniture, in which there seemed to be perpetual games of poker and craps in a constant thick fog of tobacco smoke. The fact that all activity was on the floor did not significantly diminish the density of the smoke. I went there only to get cigarettes from the very small canteen that carried a limited selection of candy bars and cigarettes. Once I stopped to kibitz a game, was asked did I want in and, knowing nothing about poker, lost and quit after two hands. In our quarters we played cards, cribbage, some chess, and did a lot of reading, everyone exchanging books with everyone else. It was not for the most part great reading, but it did kill time.

It might have been an unexciting trip overall but for the weather and the condition of the ship. The North Atlantic midwinter was rough and seasickness appeared. To make matters worse, the already aging plumbing (originally planned for East Indian waters) froze. One could still draw some water, but the sewer system was blocked up: water was rationed to a canteen a day, mostly to avoid its undisposable accumulation, and the latrines were a mess. Water mixed with sewage and vomit sloshed around in them, at times slopping over the coamings as the ship rolled.

They got things working after almost fifteen hours and it was another two or three days before things were cleaned up (by us) and back to normal. Then, about halfway over, the engines suddenly stopped, and for an interminably long and worrisome five hours we wallowed in the North Atlantic while a large escort vessel kept watch over us, circling impressively. Despite the cold, we stayed on deck the whole time and even wore life jackets without much grumbling. We caught up with the convoy late the next day.

The remainder of the trip was uneventful until we arrived in Greenock, Scotland. We knew we were close to a landfall and were proceeding in a heavy fog at a very slow speed, when suddenly the fog lifted and we had a breathtaking view of very green hillsides, houses with red tile roofs and a large bay through which we were proceeding at a slow, relaxed pace enjoying all new sights. We were full of anticipation and curiosity.

I don't remember that disembarking took very long, although it was a confused activity. I had my first cup of English tea from the Red Cross ladies on the quay. It was hot, but very strong and the evaporated milk did nothing to improve the taste; however, I did eventually develop a taste for it without milk. Sometime mid-afternoon our group was still on the quay and boarding trains. It was there I was separated from the group and directed by someone, apparently with authority, to get into a different train car. Innocent that I was, assuming all was planned (or perhaps by then well trained to obey any orders), it never occurred to me to question why this was happening and protest: I did as I was told. I also got off when told, alone, and after a brief truck ride was driven into the British 10th Replacement Depot (Lichfield Barracks). It was a large peacetime depot comprised of groups of grim buildings two or three stories high, built of dark stone, creating an effect of age, wear, and (to me) even foreboding. The buildings overlooked a large parade ground with administrative buildings on the other side, at one end of which was the large entrance gate that reinforced a feeling of captivity. I was taken directly up a dark stone staircase to a second floor landing and into a huge, dreary dormitory where our footsteps echoed on the stone floor.

It had few windows, two unlit stoves toward the ends for heat, and rows of unmade beds. I was told to bunk where I wanted, at what time formations would be, where the mess was, and my unknown guide left me alone in cavernous dreariness.

I don't know why, but I have no memory of doing anything at Lichfield other than having made up my bed since I had awakened in it the next morning (and presumably several others as well), and finally getting to talk to an efficient British Sergeant Major late in my second day. At first he was as much at a loss as I as to why I, a GI, had been assigned to a British barracks. He thankfully took on the responsibility of finding out and somehow getting me to the correct destination. It turned out that I was being quarantined in error for some unidentified illness that had affected another shipboard group. Where the quarantined group had ended up and why I was not with them remains a mystery today. I can't really remember how long I was there, though I have made an approximate calculation, based on events when I finally rejoined the group, that it was probably less than a week.

Nor have I any recollection of eating very often in the mess or any other action on my part other than going through a roll call several times, the first time without my name being called. Yet the dreary barracks room, the rough bedding that didn't look or feel too clean, the cold and dark latrines at each end of the room with their stone sinks with brass spigots from which I don't think I ever got even warm water, and the complete isolation of that second floor remain strong images. I am still surprised that after my unhappy stay of undetermined duration I don't remember any of the circumstances of my eventual departure, nor even any feeling of elation when I finally left. I do, however, remember arriving by train in London, being picked up by an American driver in a weapon's carrier, and driving around many traffic circles. I can think of no reason for this memory blackout. I don't like to think that it is due to my age (a senior moment), but I can neither imagine that the cause is some traumatic reaction nor even inattention to an unimportant event that slipped my mind.

It was raining when we drove from the station out of London to a safe house in Uxbridge. Franklin House was a pleasant, large private home with ample grounds at the end of a long driveway. It was an OSS facility staffed by GIs under a captain who maintained a very informal and, to me, luxurious ambience. I got there just before dinner and was shown to a pleasant semi-private room, and joined most of the group from which I had been separated in time for drinks. Apparently, nothing much had happened during my absence, and my stay in Lichfield Barracks aroused no interest other than being a typical SNAFU and FUBAR. Meals, served at the table by the staff, were not regular army fare but excellent; laundry was done for us, and there were no duties: it was a most pleasant change, although I had to adjust to being served by men who outranked me. Like all good things it didn't last long, though I had the opportunity to get acquainted with Uxbridge and a few trips via the underground into London. Within several days a group of us, including my brother, was scheduled to leave for training.

Our destination was Cranleigh, another large estate not too far from London, and it was not training that was involved there, but a rather extensive evaluation of each of us: psychological and motivational, determination of our ability to work as a team, and assessment of our potential for possible projected assignments. It was entirely a British operation for selection and evaluation of OSS personnel qualifications. Right from the start of our three-day stay we were constantly occupied and observed by evaluators with clipboards taking notes, asking questions at times and answering some if they pertained to the problem at hand, but otherwise never making any comment on any of our activities. While at first we were very conscious of their presence, even looking at them to see if there was any reaction to our conduct, I soon went about my activities almost completely oblivious to them.

Immediately after our arrival and having been assigned sleeping areas, we were brought to a large room, welcomed, and promised tea after we had completed a first test. It was obviously a test to determine aptitude in Morse code, consisting of pairs of combinations of dots and dashes, the objective being to determine if each pair was identical or different. With three months of learning code and a proclivity to show off, I had no difficulties at all. Others in the group who had also been in my Morse class intentionally did poorly, realizing what role a good showing would destine one for. It no doubt contributed heavily to my ultimate selection as a radio operator. After tea we were free to settle in, all the while under careful unobtrusive monitoring.

The next day the all-day sessions began. On my first session, I and five other persons I had never met were taken to a garden where there was a pond 25 to 35 foot wide. Scattered casually around were various odds and ends that might be found in a normal, very untidy yard. We were given a footlocker-size wooden crate and told the problem was to get it across the pond without us crossing. The following rules would apply. Though shallow, the pond was to be unfordable and swimming it was not permissible, nor was walking around to get to the other side. We could use anything to get it across and there was to be a three-hour time limit. The observer would answer a few questions before we started, but not after. A few of the questions asked were pertinent, ranging from 'What were the contents of the box' (not applicable to the problem; consider it classified) to 'Were the contents subject to damage by moisture' (definitely yes). After a last admonition that he would intervene only if there were an emergency, he started the clock.

There was a lively discussion of how to proceed, completely disorganized and unproductive with several loud would-be-leaders complicating everything while doing their best to take over. Several of the group chose to stand on the sidelines, sensing the futility of participation. Two of us, who thought that we should see what was available before deciding on a course of action, left the group and began collecting the odds and ends lying about. From these it was obvious that a raft had been the obvious solution chosen by previous groups. When we rejoined the heated discussion with our findings, the most verbal of the would-be-leaders immediately adopted the approach, claiming it as his own, and construction of the raft began.

With rather vociferous exchanges expressing disagreement and much fumbling around, a raft was clooged [*sic*] together. Although it held the wooden crate just barely afloat, we still had the problem of getting it across the pond. It was obvious that the raft's flotation had to be improved and that somehow it had to be gotten across the pond and unloaded. After much argument, flotation was improved sufficiently for the smallest of the group to be able to stand on the raft. We were still ardently debating how we might use poles and pieces of rope of insufficient length to get our lightest person across, how to haul the raft back, have him haul the mysterious crate back, unload it and be hauled back to the starting point when we were told our time was up. We were just coming to the conclusion that shirts, undershirts, and trousers knotted together would provide sufficient length of substitute rope. There would have remained the obstacle of getting everyone to agree to that course of action. There was no debriefing after the exercise was over. We were requested not to discuss what had transpired, even among ourselves, and I know that in my case (throughout the three days and even during my entire training) the subject of what transpired at the Cranleigh sessions never came up – even between my brother and me and close friends: perhaps we all had more promising, less personal experiences to relate. In any case, this first group was never reconstituted, and I never found myself with any of its members again during our stay.

After lunch our new group of five was introduced to our next problem. On a different part of the estate we were shown a dirt road with woods on both sides and a steep embankment dropping off into thicker woods on the far side. The lonely road constituted the frontier and was patrolled by armed guards in proper German uniforms. Our problem was to get an eight-foot wooden ladder (which was 'a critical item') across the frontier without being discovered. The area was 'verboten' to civilians like us. The rules also forbade us to attack the guard.

This time we performed as a well-coordinated and cooperative team. We had a civil, organized, and worthwhile discussion of the approaches to our problem. We voluntarily broke up into pairs to scout the 'frontier' and discover the guards' routine. We spent the necessary time observing the area, and noted, as we were no doubt intended to, that the road formed a gentle arc on the inside of which we found ourselves. The guards met roughly in the middle of the arc, chatted a short time and walked back to the ends, where their view was at best limited to past the far side of the road. It took them about five minutes to reach the end, where they always looked on up the road for some thirty seconds before turning around and beginning their return leg. Once one of them lit a cigarette, and we hoped that we could take advantage of this the next time around. That action must have been a teaser for it was never repeated.

I was in charge of the three persons elected to carry the ladder (three in case one tripped), and of giving the signal to make the run across the road when the other two members of our group, each watching one of the guards, signaled that one of the guards was making his turn. I had to wait several tense routines before both guards reached the end of their territory together before giving the signal to go, permitting everyone to scurry across unseen. Again there was no discussion or any indication given of the success of this team performance.

The next morning was spent on more individual tests involving some minor problem-solving and decision-making. This gave the staff an opportunity to evaluate us individually more closely, although we were all clearly identified by large numbers. Given a goal of accumulating fifty points, for example, I was given (and assume all the others were too) a set of decisions involving some degree of choosing between risk and accomplishment, depending on one's physical abilities and agility. For example, crossing a theoretical pool of acid using randomly spaced wooden stumps about six to eight inches in diameter might be worth six points. Moving on similar sized stumps, but which were off the ground by one to three feet and still randomly spaced far enough apart to make a stretching long hop necessary, made it very difficult, if not almost impossible, to stop on any one in order to gauge the next move. Going over this 'course' when the height of each subsequent stump increased was relatively easy: going down was much more scary and difficult. After each of six such tasks we were asked why we had chosen that particular one, the answers in my case being that they either seemed interesting, were challenging but feasible, or most often represented the most points. There were also many other leading questions, some pertaining to what we would like to be training for (no known preference since existing options were not identified or defined), others dealing with whether there were any persons with whom we would not like to have to run risks, either as companions or for other reasons. For some thoughtless or perhaps subconscious reason, I named Pierre (he being my mother's favorite and wanting to please, I suppose), explaining that risking one member of the family was enough. He never did get the chance to jump in. I don't know whether that statement of mine was a determining factor in his never being selected for an operation or whether there were other reasons for his serving only as an OSS home station operator ending up in Germany. I never ran into him all the time we were in England, nor indeed saw him again until several years after the war, and by then our relationship had changed and I never felt free to tell him or anyone else what I had done. I have always regretted that action very much. It was a god-like decision on a matter that did not involve me.

The problem on the last day was geared entirely to the individual. The situation I was presented with was as follows: you are part of an underground network, one of whose members has been arrested. There are some compromising papers hidden in his room. Find them and get them out. The person giving the instructions for the problem also acted the part of a very nervous and pushy fellow underground member. I should have insisted more emphatically on specific background information, on the relationship between us, the layout of the location I was to operate in, the size and quantity of the compromising papers, and even the criticality of the need for action. When I started to ask questions, he professed to know nothing more, not even what the compromising papers consisted of or their quantity, and he continued urging immediate action, even pushing me. In retrospect, I should have stuck to getting more information and not let him pressure me and, I suppose, he might have answered questions if I had categorically insisted before being willing to act. It was soon obvious that the reaction to that discussion, I am now quite certain, had to be the heart of the evaluation. But tense, immature, and inexperienced as I was, I accepted far too unquestioningly the urgency of the scenario. Other than knowing I was looking for perhaps a couple of sheets of paper, that the arrest had occurred the previous day, and that the other would act as lookout, I foolishly went ahead almost completely blind.

I went to the room, the second door from the end of the corridor on the right at the top of the stairs, as directed. It was a fully furnished room with a bed, a dresser, a desk and chair, an easy chair, several bookshelves and there were many books and magazines lying about. I immediately started searching the underside of drawers, a location stressed somewhere in the OSS training. I was starting to look behind the books on the shelves when the lookout came bursting in announcing that the German police were coming up the stairs. I suggested walking down the stairs as if I were a resident, but he was emphatic that the concierge was with them and would not identify me as a tenant. I next proposed going to the far end of the hall and acting as if I were about to enter my apartment, or of taking on the role of being a thief breaking into whatever rooms were open, burglary being a far lesser offense than espionage. I was looking for something to take for cover when I realized that my lookout had been urgently pressing, almost pushing me toward the window, urging me to go out of it, along the roof past the dormer at the end of the building and down a fire escape ladder that was just around the end of the building. I lost control of the situation being unable to think of an alternative action, not even something as basic as asking him how he was getting out, nor telling him to go, that there was no sense in both of us being found. I could not get him to listen to me and ended up following his instructions, though to this day I can only explain it as a momentary panic engendered by his excellent acting and my complete inexperience and immaturity.

I did think of trying the end dormer window to see if I could re-enter the building, but it was locked and I didn't feel I should break the window. Instead, I crept and crawled along a small ledge that held up the gutters and tried not to look down at the ground three stories below.

The metal ladder also posed a problem for there was not much to grasp getting onto it. I was much annoyed at myself for the unquestioning acceptance of instructions and equally disappointed with my performance. The lack of any comment or expression as I was met at the foot of the ladder, other than the now-expected instructions not to mention the test, only accentuated my sense of complete failure as I was escorted to the mess hall. We all returned to Uxbridge shortly after lunch following a farewell speech telling us, somewhat tongue in cheek, that it was hoped we had enjoyed and benefited from our stay at Cranleigh.

After some four or five days in Franklin House, spent exploring Uxbridge and London via the Underground, and trying to forget the Cranleigh experience (but, strangely enough, still not discussing it with anyone), I was told to report to an address on Baker Street. Found it without much difficulty. It was not an old brownstone à la Sherlock Holmes as I half fancied it might be, but a very plain office building. Inside the small lobby a guard asked me to sign in and directed me to an upper floor where I was met on the landing and escorted to a small, plain sparsely furnished office. There I was interviewed briefly by several men, some in uniform and others not. It was more an introduction into the organization than a formal interview, although my French was tested by one of them. It has been reported that Colonel Buckmaster (Head of the Special Operations Executive, SOE) made the effort to meet all the personnel in his organization; I can assume that one of the persons with whom I talked that day was him, though I can claim no personal memory of any such identification. Later, the leader of the team I finally joined mentioned that while waiting for final go-ahead for the operation, Buckmaster had told them all that he had found an American radio operator for them.

Be that as it may, other than filling out a few forms and providing some current data to a very efficient and kind lady, a Mrs. Norris, with whom I interfaced almost exclusively thereafter, the only recollection I have of the entire meeting was the announcement that I would be shortly going to some schools for further training, and the awareness that I would now somehow be separated from Franklin House. Indeed, I never had contact with any of my former group, including my brother. Over the next several days, when not regularly checking in with Baker Street, I spent most of my time wandering about London as a very uninformed and sometimes bored tourist, staying in a small, inexpensive hotel. I got used to walking in blacked-out streets and even being accosted by the numerous and active Piccadilly Commandos, though never having the nerve or the money to follow through. I also managed one very enjoyable excursion, a visit to Windsor Castle.

Without much advance notice I found myself one afternoon on a train for Scotland. I had been told I would be met by someone at some place called Morar, where I would receive some commando-type training. After a rather long, packed, and blacked-out train ride with an intermediate change in a big darkened city that I can't now identify (but must have been Glasgow), I found myself on a virtually empty train to Fort William and entirely alone from there to Morar. On getting off onto the very dimly lit quay in heavy Scottish mist, and being unable to see anyone around, I had a few moments of doubt because there did not seem to be another building of any kind anywhere nearby. However, after a long five minutes, a small lorry appeared and the driver picked me up with a casual but friendly greeting. No identification was requested and in view of the locale was obviously not necessary. I was taken directly to the training area, passing a small cluster of houses shortly after leaving the station, but no other habitations for the several miles to our destination.

A rather large, somewhat remodeled farmhouse served as the mess and recreation area and, I believe, housed the staff and instructors. Close by were several other buildings, obviously new additions, in one of which we were housed, the others being for storage of equipment and other unknown purposes. It was after 7 p.m. when I got there, but I was formally greeted by the officer of the day, fed and introduced to some of the other trainees, and then shown where I would sleep, after being informed that the training would start first thing in the morning.

The next morning, immediately upon arising, I was issued a British battledress uniform, told to put it on and fall out for the 'morning stroll'. This turned out to involve pairing off with a random partner, picking up a log eight feet long and eight inches in diameter, and starting off at a fast pace with periods of jogging to 'keep us awake'. After a good hour of this, sometimes on a narrow hilly road, other times cross-country, we returned home for the balance of the training day. We did this every morning. The log was rather heavy and awkward to carry, especially at first, and required that we, the bearers, learn to travel at the same speed and rhythm of step, as well as making sure each understood when and how to shift the load, involving both the method and side of portage. The first day I got a painful case of shin splints which took most of the rest of the training session to overcome. The 'stroll' logs went with us everywhere to different training sites and courses, waiting where we had put them down for other activities, until it was time to pick them up for another activity or bring them home after the training session.

After the 'stroll' we were occupied with training in many weapons (primarily US and German), demolition (specifically the use of British explosives and for particular applications such as culverts and small steel bridges), and some hand-to-hand combat. The primary emphasis, however, was on small group movement, getting from point A to point B as invisibly as possible while overcoming specific obstacles. Relative invisibility was not always easy in the open Scottish highlands, and the exercises were made more difficult by artificial impediments imposed by the staff. For instance, a small stream we could easily have crossed scarcely getting our feet wet was decreed to require the use of a rope conveniently stretched (not tautly) between two trees. This we were to accomplish by lying on the rope with one leg dangling down for balance, as we had been lectured the previous day. Apparently, the lecture had not been absorbed by all of us, since some of our group insisted on doing it hand-over-hand hanging from the rope, swinging back and forth with their equipment impeding their movements. Only a few made across it in that manner, the others dropping off, unable to hang on. The rest of us, at first untrusting, managed to lie gingerly on the rope and haul ourselves to the other end in spite of the equipment that complicated smooth movement. It was a much less strenuous and easier way to get across than the hand-over-hand way, where all the weight was on the wrists. The only abnormal incident that occurred during our stay was when someone tossed a quarter pound block of TNT into one of the many streams and killed two good-sized salmon. We were given a stern lecture about sportsmanship and an apology was conveyed to the owner of the stream, but we did get to eat the salmon.

Evenings were mostly spent 'at home'. Drinks were available and some disparate reading materials, but most of the time we were all very tired and in bed early. The exceptions were two night exercises, one involving comprehensive reception committee training. Also two Belgians and I spent several evenings until after ten o'clock with an officer on the staff who was translating into French instructions on how to disassemble, clean, and reassemble various weapons. The three of us had the same problem: we could clearly translate the actions to be performed but knew none of the nomenclature of the parts, even such simple ones as 'trigger' or 'bolt'. As I look back on this, I realize that this must have been a test since the matter of such translations had obviously been taken care of by early 1944, although at the time it never occurred to me and we all tried to be as helpful as we could. The officer we were 'helping' was perfectly fluent in French, and the Free French forces would have provided all the technical assistance needed, indeed they would have been much more helpful than us.

I do not remember the return trip to London, nor much of the random inactivity I suffered in and around London during the short leave I was given upon my return, other than a trip to Cambridge, visits to several museums, Madame Tussauds wax works, several time-killing movies and, of course, the bland food in the inexpensive restaurants my pay forced me to patronize. There were two exceptional evenings: having picked up two women in a pub, I had to break off accompanying them home to take care of my companion, who had drunk too much gin and orange and passed out; and the other of a night out with an Italian-American OSS companion to Frascati's, a rather posh restaurant, where the lamb chops turned out to be mutton and tasted like soap.

Within the week training resumed, and I had been assigned to Thame Park, a beautiful small estate where I spent (as well as I can remember) the next six to eight weeks. It was a genteel routine, quite different from the Morar experience: I was awoken by a batman with the first cup of tea, down to breakfast, which differed little from normal army fare, followed by courses with a nice break for lunch, more courses, followed by a sort of high tea that served as dinner, leaving the evenings free. The only drawback for me was the constant, all-pervasive chill. The warmest place was the mess hall (where I still remember relishing tea-time slices of toast fried in bacon fat). There were radiators throughout but they were never on, and while there was usually a small fire in the fireplace in the 'recreation' room, it didn't stand a chance of heating the space that in better days must have been a stunning drawing room. The local village pub, about a mile away, was much more inviting, active, and warmer. We frequented it with regularity, and no one ever questioned our presence or showed the slightest curiosity about the mix of accents and uniforms.

Initially, the training involved increasing our speed in sending and receiving Morse code, but after we had mastered a solid twenty-five words per minute, a word being a five-letter group of random letters with the occasional inclusion of some numbers, we were introduced to the operational procedure we would be using. It was basically a commercial procedure with commercial Q signals (which abbreviated the necessary communications involved in making and ending contacts), the intent being to enable us to pass ourselves off, at least for a brief, initial period, as ordinary, everyday transmissions. When we became very familiar with that, we were introduced to the sets we would use.

Until then, all of the sending and receiving practice had been artificial, static-free, on a closed circuit, as it had been in Area C in Maryland, but now we listened to real transmissions and when we practiced tuning the transmitter we were in fact sending. Tuning emitted a steady signal, and speed was emphasized in performing this function to minimize the danger of discovery by DF (Direction Finding). Message transmission should, if at all possible, be limited to five minutes on any one frequency. This was about the extent to which the subject of German DF was ever covered; no details of its methodology and its efficiency nor, understandably, any mention of the average operational life of WT operators (some six to eight weeks for those working in an urban post, according to post-war hearsay).

As I learned long after the war from Pierre Lorain's *Clandestine Operations*, the German DFing was fast, efficient, and lethal. By 1944, it could triangulate the position of a transmitting set in about fourteen minutes from a DFing central in Paris. The central had some 300 receiver stations fitted with television-like cathode ray tubes, each receiver covering all traffic on a 100 kilocycle band under German control or from abroad, each frequency displayed as a luminous spot. Any new operating frequency would immediately show up as an unidentified spot. The new frequency would be called in to three DF stations outside of France or on its periphery that would triangulate on that frequency, locating it within a ten-mile triangle. At that point, mobile DFing equipment (in conjunction with a fixed DF station in the general area of the first triangulation) moved in, cars taking positions at the intersection of two of the peripheral stations' azimuths. The result was a new triangle of sides up to 1 mile long, within which the new station was located. Three vehicles at the apex of this triangle located the transmission to within 200 yards. The final effort was accomplished by pedestrian-held field-strength meters.

The set we were to use to operate in this unknown DFing environment was contained in a small attaché-type case, about 18 by
13 by 5 inches, a Type B Mark II set (although I find it difficult to
understand why I have retained that bit of data). It was comprised of
three parts: a power supply that worked on a variety of DC and AC
voltages, a receiver that was very sensitive, and a transmitter whose
operation depended on crystals to establish the frequencies to be
used. It was a little heavy to carry casually as one would a normal
briefcase, but it had a range of some 500 miles. After we became
adept at the critical task of tuning it quickly to avoid emitting an
easy-to-detect, steady signal, we received an introduction on its
maintenance and repair. This was not presented with vigor, was too
theoretical for many of us, and was considerably beyond the interest
and comprehension of most, so we tended to ignore it, all the more
since the reliability of the set was constantly and heavily emphasized.
After several sessions on wave lengths and antenna placement we
were, I suppose, thought to be sufficiently trained.

There remained some summary training in encoding and decoding with a simple, but effective, double transposition method. This
involved writing the message letter for letter under the letters provided from furnished five-letter groups. Then using a conversion
sheet with columns of random letters under headings A through Z
across the top and rows A through Z headings down on the left-
hand side, the first upper letter from the combined five-letter group
was matched with the same one in the top horizontal heading, and
the first letter of text below it was matched with the equivalent one
from the vertical heading, thereby obtaining a resulting transposed
letter at the point where the horizontal and vertical met.

The task of repeating this process for each letter of the message
was slow and tedious, although in time one learned most of the
combinations by heart. The only problem was that the sheets of
five-letter groups used in training were regular typewritten fonts,
while in the field they were printed on microfiches 4 inches by
4 inches each containing a thousand groups, and the transposing
sheet was printed on silk some 4 inches by 6 inches. A separate set

of microfiches was used for sending and for receiving messages. As I look at them now, they are indeed very difficult to read. For some security reason, the operational silk provided was different from the training one, and I had to unlearn the combinations that had become familiar in training.

We had been told that as a final exam we would be expected to go to an English city with a set, get a room, and meet a schedule of transmissions without, hopefully, being detected. I assume it was due to more pressing requirements that I never underwent the test and instead was almost immediately sent to Ringway, in the greater outer suburbs south of Manchester, for parachute training. For the first time I became aware that I never encountered any fellow trainees from previous sessions. I don't know whether this was planned or coincidental, but new places always seemed to mean new faces.

The installation at Ringway was, in fact, merely a rather large home just off a main road with a large yard, a tall two-story garage with a large cupola, shrubbery, and a wall running around the entire property. There were perhaps slightly more than a dozen of us, and immediately after being shown our quarters, we were taught how to fall; keeping legs together slightly bent, hands above our heads, rolling to the right or left side, the shock of the fall being absorbed by the roll. We did this for several hours, and then continued the same exercise holding onto a bar which hung from a small wheel riding a cable that sloped toward the ground from a twelve-foot starting height, doing our roll with momentum when our feet hit the ground, adding a degree of reality to the 'landing'.

More of the same the next morning, followed by jumping in a harness. For this we went up to the second floor of the garage, in which a four-foot round hole had been cut. The harness was attached to a cable unwinding from a small drum fixed in the cupola. Two small paddles were attached on the opposite sides of the drum, perpendicular to its rotation when the cable unwound. With the easy, laid-back, this-is-fun approach used during this particular training session, there was no demonstration of how we were not to be maimed in the two-and-a-half-story fall to the ground. Hard as it was for us to believe at first, those two little paddles whirled faster as the cable played out and the diameter of the drum shrank, and succeeded in slowing the descent, after an initial sense of free fall, to a perfectly acceptable landing impact.

The real purpose of this part of the training was twofold. First, to familiarize us with the harness and risers, which ones to pull on to direct or collapse a parachute, and particularly the turn-and-press-to-release mechanism which automatically freed one from the harness. This handy gadget had not yet been adopted by the US. It was thought to be unreliable and a possible cause of unexpected releases, although by eliminating the need to unhook four clips near the groin at the end of the harness straps upon landing, it allowed immediate, easy release from the 'chute. Then, more importantly, the second part of the training was to teach us how to exit the plane British-style through a round hole in the floor, instead of the US way through a side door.

So we practiced sitting around the edge of it, swiveled our feet into it on the command 'action stations', and pushed upwards and out at 'go'. We had several practice exits, enough to feel we knew the drill. Before tea we were taken to watch the packing of the 'chutes to give us confidence, we were told, since we would have no reserve 'chute, and in fact didn't need one since we wouldn't have time to use one at the low altitude at which we would be jumping.

Early the next morning, dressed in jumpsuits, we were taken by bus to an airport, where we boarded an old Whitley bomber. There was a certain lack of joking and a general silence among the students. It was the first time in my life that I had been in an airplane. We went out in sticks of two (so the instructors on the ground could better monitor how we did on our descent). Our mental conditioning through the this-is-fun ambience of the training paid off. I felt only the mildest tension on the 'action station' command, when I could see the ground past my feet through the hole, and an easy push off on 'go'. A slight jerk when the 'chute was pulled open by the static line (for the Whitley was old and slow) confirmed that the 'chute had opened, and there followed an exhilarating feeling of floating with no downward motion over a quiet landscape. Loudspeaker instructions from the ground attracted my attention though I paid little attention to what was being said, mesmerized by the sensation of weightlessness; but then I suddenly realized that the ground was coming up at me very quickly. I scarcely had time to react when I touched the ground, so lightly that I had to force myself to tumble. The 'chute collapsed easily and, very satisfied, I bundled it up and walked to the edge of the field, where my enthusiasm for the apparently motionless hanging was duplicated by all present.

In the critique we were all told our performance was adequate for a first jump, but that we should pay more attention to getting ready for the end of the short trip down. We had been fortunate with the total lack of wind, not even a breeze; in fact, a small female trainee had had the unusual problem of not being heavy enough to fully counteract the light morning updraft and had a frustratingly slow and most irregular descent.

The next morning we took off again, this time full of confidence in our abilities, lustily singing raunchy songs in the bus. That day there was some wind and I could see the ground moving diagonally under me because of it as I sat by the hole awaiting my turn. I didn't daydream on my way down. The landing was hard since I had not gauged the swing of my body in relation to the 'chute, and was in the air at the end of an arc when my feet should have been just touching the ground. While I managed to roll I landed with a thump. I had not been pulling on the proper risers to minimize the swing. I also had the totally new experience of collapsing my 'chute in a quite gentle breeze, and was impressed by its effect on the 'chute. After lunch we returned to the Whitley and made our third jump. The wind was the same, but I managed to perform the correct maneuvers and made my best landing, easily collapsing the 'chute.

On our last day we saw a film on the handling of risers, getting down from landings in a tree, collapsing 'chutes, gathering them up into a bundle that would be easy to handle or dispose of, and were briefed for a night jump that evening. This time it was not from a Whitley but from a tethered balloon with a gondola large enough to hold six of us and with the requisite hole in the floor. As we were let up, we could see small dim blue lights spaced along the cable, but the ground was invisible; there was no moon. The accompanying dispatcher checked to make sure the static lines were clipped on, then casually, as if reviewing things, said, 'You chaps know the drill well enough so you don't need me,' and jumped. It was a difficult adjustment to issue the jump commands to oneself rather than simply reacting obediently. I decided I didn't want to be last and went out in the first stick. Without the slipstream from a plane's momentum, there was a very sickening, unexpected feeling of free fall, then in the silence I could hear my 'chute snap open with a sharp crack, but I don't remember seeing the ground until seconds before I landed. I rolled properly in a relatively soft landing. Having bundled my 'chute as we had seen in the film, I started walking toward voices, since I was completely disoriented, as, it turned out, were the owners of the voices, and the three of us eventually made our way back to the bus. After a little celebration of the course's conclusion that night, during which we were congratulated as now qualified parachutists, I left for London the next morning.

This time I was sent for a number of short stays in a holding area near London where I had some free time to play volleyball when I wasn't being hustled about with a myriad varied tasks. It was there that I formed a friendship with a member of the opposing volleyball team whose English was that of a Frenchman. He was my age, easy-going, and not afraid to use his Parisian slang. He was a *sportif* ('jock' is perhaps the nearest current equivalent though without all the pejorative implications of the English). We spent much of our time in the holding area together, speaking French, and while we did not discuss anything personal, we got along very well, seemed to have much in common (particularly our outlook on life), and developed a good relationship that was closer and had more informality than I had enjoyed so far, or was common in training sessions. I knew him only as Bob, and by coincidence the only other trainee with whom I had had such a relationship had also been named Bob, at Thame Park. This Bob was not as busy as I, and it seemed to me that I spent my time shifting quarters and shuttling between the holding area, the Welbec office, and other London locations. I was acutely aware that things were really starting to happen in those two following weeks.

Almost immediately I was questioned about how I presently felt about soon being activated, which came as no surprise but nonetheless required a facing of reality. I again formally declared my willingness to proceed with the little thought for the various possible consequences that only the confidence of unthinking youth can provide. After I had received a somewhat cursory physical examination, one of the first steps in the activation process was the preparation of a last will and testament, which was a little disconcerting for an optimist who had just turned twenty, the more so since I had very little to will. Then I was escorted to an old, derelict-looking warehouse of a shop where tailors with strong foreign accents coached me in choosing appropriate current French civilian clothing; everything from underwear, socks, handkerchiefs, shirts, trousers, shoes, and jacket. As yet I was aware of neither my cover story nor any operational destination, but it was obvious to the professional personnel in that shop what type and quality of clothing a young man my age should wear in order not to stand out or attract notice. The clothes would be aged and, if necessary due to operational requirements, could be changed and even have labels sewn on. Several days later, when I returned to pick up my things, they all looked like I had lived in them for a long time, somewhat used and often laundered but, when inspected closely, they were not at all worn out. The shiny new leather jacket and the shoes had lost all their gloss and stiff newness for a faded and somewhat scuffed and flexible appearance.

In the meantime I had spent some time providing information and helping to develop my cover story. There was a certain logic to it. My name was changed from Jean Claude Guiet to Claude Jean Guyot in order to keep the sounds fairly familiar. A birth certificate showed that I was born in Gouvieux, north of Paris, on my real birthday of 15 March, but it gave my birth year as 1917, aging me by seven years. This allowed for a military service discharge as a corporal from the

81st Battalion of Alpine Fortress Infantry in Draguignan on 24 July 1940. I had joined in Lons-le-Saunier (a town I knew very well, having lived in the area for five years before the war and attended the *lycée* there in 1939–40), and prior to that had lived at 22 avenue du Maréchal Pétain, Bourg-en-Bresse, Ain (with which I was also quite familiar). A census form showed me residing there in February 1943, my food and clothing ration cards had both been issued there in August 1942. However, by April 1943, I had moved to Toulouse and was occupied as an office boy as I had been before in Bourg-en-Bresse. I lived at 30 rue Denfert Rochereau and my employer was Mr Jean Leygue, an agronomy engineer who involved me in a job whose manual aspects I disliked. I was told that he might vaguely remember someone like me working for him, but would provide no recommendations or identification.

I had all the appropriate papers for all this fictional history, duly signed and stamped, written in a variety of different inks and hands, appearing well-used, and bearing my fingerprints and signature where required. My parents' involvement was limited: my father became René Guyot, who had died in Senlis in 1930, and my mother, Jeanne Seigneur, who had taken up with several lovers, had become quite an alcoholic. I had broken contact with her and didn't know or care particularly where she was. The last reports, dating back to the start of my military service, were that she had returned to the Senlis area. I had left Toulouse temporarily to seek other employment. My parents' real first names and my mother's maiden name were used to make it easier for me to retain as much information as possible, thereby reducing the possibility of slip ups. I was also briefed on the peculiarities of specific places I had supposedly been in, for example the railroad station in Marseilles, through which I would have passed upon my army discharge. It was indeed as the briefing had depicted it when I saw it some twenty-five years after the war. While these papers would withstand a cursory or even a brief routine check, they were not intended to hold up to more than that. They were not like those of one fortunate individual, prepared with the full collaboration of the local bureaucracy, which were in fact the documents of an unreported deceased relative, their every detail verifiable and backed by family.

The day after I selected my clothing, I had been taken to some US installation and received an honorable discharge as a corporal, dated 19 May, and within the hour a commission as a 2nd Lieutenant dated 20 May. I was anticipating going out to buy my new uniform the next day, but instead was told to report back to the Baker Street office. There I was shown into the usual almost bare office space and was presented to a British Major who introduced himself as Major Charles Staunton. He appeared to me to be perhaps in his late thirties, was slightly shorter than I, had a rather olive complexion and somewhat bulging eyes which shone, alert and friendly.

We started the interview in English, him speaking in the classic British accent, but then he took me quite aback when he switched to French, speaking with what was definitely a perfect Parisian accent. After a brief period of very general and informal questioning and conversation, he expressed relief and satisfaction that my French was native, unlike that of many of his other candidates, said I seemed to fit his requirements well and was certain we would work well together. He did allow that he was indeed French when I asked, and invited me to lunch.

When we entered the crowded Soho restaurant, a long, narrow, very noisy room full of French military and naval personnel, I was surprised again, this time by a pseudo-formal introduction to a Bob Mortier, the same Bob with whom I had played volleyball during free time in the holding area. To my surprise, in violation, I thought, of security, he and Staunton made no effort to blend with their British uniforms and spoke nonchalantly in their native Parisian accents. They were obviously close friends and Bob, with his Clark Gable mustache and the cap of his Canadian Captain's uniform set at a cocky angle, assumed a devil-may-care attitude. Until then I had only seen him in nondescript clothing. We managed a short-lived formal greeting, but quickly dropped the fiction of not having met before. From their comments as the conversation developed, I gathered that Bob had played some role in my selection.

We had scarcely finished 'meeting' when a very attractive FANY (first aid nursing yeomanry) officer joined us. They all knew each other well and she was introduced to me as Corinne. She, too, seemed to be my age, was pleasantly informal, vivacious, and lively, and struck me as very attractive with a round face, eyes that seemed to squint a little and long dark hair over a rather high forehead. She was not very tall, perhaps a few inches over five feet, seemed very lithe, moved with a smooth grace and seemed to take everything with casual ease and humor. Her French, while perfect, had a trace of an accent which might have caught the ear of a very suspicious person, and, more surprisingly, she spoke English with what seemed to my quite untrained ear a slight cockney-like accent, especially noticeable when compared to Bob's or Staunton's accents.

We had a pleasant lunch, in spite of the hubbub, conversation being limited to broad, general topics, but relaxed and friendly and they made frequent allusions to past events in their lives. The little personal information discussed was mine as they sought to get to know me better.

Major Staunton no doubt had been thoroughly acquainted with my background but showed no sign of it. It was obvious from their conduct that they knew each other and worked well together, and that they had had many experiences together. Through no fault of theirs I could not help but feel a late-comer to the group, and indeed this feeling, almost of inferiority, was perhaps even accentuated in my mind by my lack of visible rank and the haphazard uniform I was then wearing, and did little to reduce an exaggerated natural shyness. To all this, youthful inexperience and a desire not to show any poor security consciousness further made me ill at ease and precluded my asking many questions. There was no mention of any upcoming operation, our role, its timing, or its location. It was only in October, when they were in Paris and I was on my way back to London, that I finally learned that their new operation had just been approved and learned their real names. Charles Staunton, whom I called Charles throughout the operation, was Philippe Liewer; Bob Mortier was really Bob Maloubier; Corinne was Violette Szabó.

In the next few days I had no opportunity to get together with my new teammates. I had a little time to go buy my new officer's uniform, and made several visits to the Post Exchange before I at last had to take the only raincoat available, which was several sizes too large. I had finally gotten those longed-for jump boots. I spent several long and tedious evenings placing and sewing insignia on cap and shirt, which fit, but I never got to wear the uniform as the adjustments to the trousers took almost a week.

So I went, still as a corporal for several days, then as an officer in enlisted man's olive drab, from one last-minute assignment to another, each apparently requiring more things to remember and decide. It seemed to me that almost at once I was requested to pack all the things I owned for storage during my 'absence', including the new uniform, which went directly from the tailor to the suitcase. I remember nothing of being given any specific information as to the mission in which I was to participate, and while not particularly concerned whether my cover story was adequate, I was very aware that I needed more detailed explanations of exactly how and for what purpose each of the false papers I had been given (particularly the ration books) were to be used. I expressed my concern to Mrs Norris in the office and a meeting with SOE personnel was set up.

My false papers were again clearly explained, including a short training session in which I was peremptorily asked to show certain papers. This was followed by a familiarization session with my ration books, which provided very useful clarification concerning both what I had already consumed and what I had yet coming. However, I believe I still knew virtually nothing about any specific forthcoming operation. I found out much later that it was still in the final stages of being set up. I also made the decision not to accept a poison pill I was offered in case of capture; I wrote some four or five very poor letters (advance-dated at periodic intervals) to be sent to my parents, which did not fool them; I arranged that all but the current month's pay be deposited to a bank account; I had several sessions with radio people who wanted to make sure, with me present, that my new set was complete; I was given transmission security briefings; I was shown my coding microfiche with its miniscule print for the first time; and I was instructed how to cut off and destroy all the coding groups that had been used (with a small pair of scissors included in the set). Also stressed (needlessly, I thought) was that the Home Station microfiche was used for decoding and the Out Station fiche for encoding. I was also given my security signals, which were to be included in every message to show that I was not transmitting under duress. Finally, I was given a worn-looking suitcase in which I packed my civilian clothing.

CHAPTER 3

I don't know whether it was due to the confusion of those last weeks or an unfelt subconscious tension regarding what might be forthcoming, but I don't remember clearly much of the few days that preceded the first or second of June 1944. I know that, due to my busy schedule, I had no further contact with the three persons I had recently met. Difficult as it is to believe, I don't remember any briefing on our destination, nor even any mention of it. But someone must have briefed me on where we were headed, if not the precise nature of our mission, since it seems absolutely inconceivable that I could be expected to drop into a location without any advance knowledge of it, though I have no recollection whatsoever of ever having been told. I do recall there had been a last-minute change in our destination due to some troubles in that particular area of operation. This turned out to have been the capture of the leader and roll up of much of the entire stationer organization in the area into which we had been scheduled to jump. Surprisingly, I don't remember being very troubled by the news. It was almost as if it did not concern me.

That I was in no way surprised on our arrival in the Haute Vienne would indicate that I had been told where I was headed. I had also assumed I was driven to Tempsford air base with Bob and Charles

Staunton, though I have since been told that agents were always driven separately. I do remember Corinne arriving separately shortly after us, accompanied, if I remember correctly, by Nancy Fraser Campbell from the Orchard Street office, and that also a Vera Atkins was present just before departure. I am uncertain whether we went to a large dormitory-like house or directly to the air base. I know we had a meal and do distinctly remember the final checkout in a barn-like room just off the tarmac, where we changed into our civilian clothes and jumpsuits. Our clothes, as well as our wallets and papers, were all inspected and checked for any possible idiosyncrasies or non-French items which might compromise us, as were our suitcases before they were packed to be dropped with us.

My schedules and coding material were to be carried on my person, in a hidden compartment of my wallet: the crystals were verified again against the schedule requirements and put in a small cardboard box to be carried on my person. We slipped into our lightweight jumpsuits, pocketed our pistols, and, just before leaving the area, were informed that we would be going through Customs, a mere formality we were assured, and were not to declare that we had weapons. Feeling the absurdity of the situation, we all quietly walked through Customs as if it were the most normal thing in the world for four luggage-less civilians in jumpsuits to be asked very politely if they had anything to declare as they passed through to the dark and blustery tarmac to a waiting airplane. We passed through with no trouble, as expected, and our discussion of whether anyone had ever been stopped from passing and on what grounds such action might occur was a somewhat tension-inducing diversion as we were being driven to the airplane.

We climbed into the plane, an RAF bomber called, if I remember correctly, *C for Charlie*, whose dispatcher helped us up, showed us our places, checked our 'chutes, and tried to make us feel at ease as he settled us on the floor in the dark while the plane started to move. Then, after a few minutes it stopped. We all assumed it was waiting for clearance for takeoff until the dispatcher informed us the flight had been scratched due to bad weather. I think we were all very much disappointed at this turn of events: I know I certainly was. For me there was a strong sense of anticlimax, disgruntlement, and almost anger that things had not gone as planned. In retrospect, there probably was also some not so subconscious apprehension at having still to accomplish what hadn't been done.

In that mood we climbed out of the plane, and were driven to and lodged in Hazells Hall after again going through the charade of passing through Customs, although this time it had lost its comic relief. Corinne had her own room down the hall while we three men shared a spacious room and alcove. I don't recall we expressed our feelings then, other than declaring that we had really been ready to go, that we no longer felt much tension, that tomorrow would be the day, and let's get some rest, which we did after having a drink as we tiredly sang what was to become our group theme song – 'I'll Be Around' – ('I'll be around no matter how you treat me now, I'll be around from now on …').

Hazells Hall, a huge Georgian building, was filled with SOE personnel of various types, mostly Jedburgh teams of some three or four allied members who were destined to drop in in uniform and organize resistance and disruption. We had our breakfast fairly early in the dining hall, after which Staunton (having established that we were free of any official obligations) decided that we didn't want to have to kill the whole day at Hazells Hall. We borrowed a car from the staff and the four of us drove to Cambridge, where we strolled about and had a pleasant lunch, returning to Hazells Hall in the mid-afternoon. To kill time until departure preparations, we played ping-pong and interminable games of blackjack, making reckless bets with the British money we would no longer need. Corinne seemed to win the majority of the time yet, strangely enough, none of us came out a significant winner and since we all owed each other, our 'I'll Be Around' song got a lot of mileage as a sort of jocular implied guarantee of payment and cohesion.

We again went through Customs, after the routine of checking clothing and papers, but it was now so routine as to elicit no comic relief or comment, and boarded an RAF plane – I think a Lancaster bomber. We were a rather quiet group this time, and I certainly didn't feel the sense of anticipation and exhilaration of the previous boarding. This time we took off. We were helped into our 'chutes and sat in the dark not doing much talking (what there was of it was quite subdued), played some more blackjack, gratefully accepted the coffee and hot chocolate offered by the dispatcher, and tried to doze.

All at once, the somewhat somnolent atmosphere disappeared as a standby warning light came on and we checked our 'chutes. My prime concern, totally preoccupying me at that moment, was the possibility that I might lose my small cardboard box with its precious crystals, key to our communications. It kept sliding around under the harness straps, and I could neither move it to a position where the harness would keep it in place nor tighten the harness sufficiently to solve the problem, in spite of having it so tight that I was forced into a very uncomfortable slouch. I had visions of it free-falling and the crystals scattering to the ground, and being responsible for the failure of the entire operation.

While I wrestled in panic to solve my problem, the cover was removed from the hole and we sat around the edge looking down at the dark landscape, scarcely lit by a dim moon, passing below us. We exchanged glances of encouragement, but our attention was on the ground below. I know I was very tense, as was Charles sitting to my right. I watched the muscles of his jaw twitch and was a little reassured that someone who had gone in before was nervous too. It was only much later that I discovered that this was also his first operation jump, his prior arrivals and departures in France being by Lysander, a small plane similar to a Piper Cub. For what seemed an endless stretch of time, but was probably no more than five to ten minutes, the plane made several passes over the area. With each pass we caught glimpses of the landscape on which we were to land. We passed over many woods, hills, some fields and meadows, a few small streams reflecting what little light the moon furnished, even a darkened village or two.

As we circled, any elation I felt at the thought of jumping diminished, a reaction that was shared by all the others, as I afterwards discovered. A final, brief moment of anxiety brought an end to the strain when the dispatcher moved closer to us as if to send us on our way, before we realized that it was to inform us that no jump was to occur. He motioned us over out of the way and we watched as some caged carrier pigeons and pamphlets were dropped through the hole at pre-specified points on the way back before he closed the hole for the remainder of the trip home. I always wondered how many of those pigeons made it home or ended up in some French pot.

The dispatcher made sympathetic comments regretting that all our difficult preparations had been in vain as he helped us settle down with loosened harnesses for the return trip. There was an almost palpable degree of relaxation on my part, a literal lifting of a burden, and from the renewal of a near-normal liveliness among us all, it was obvious that we all experienced a high degree of relief. The trip back seemed definitely shorter than the outward bound one. When the dispatcher let us know that we would soon be home, I happened to mention that when we landed it would be the first time I had ever landed in an airplane. He contacted the pilot and just as a faint pre-dawn became noticeable in the sky, the ground still dark, I was taken for a short visit to the bombardier's station in the nose in time to see the English countryside slowly sloping up toward me in the breaking dawn right until we touched down. I was very impressed. Obviously recovered from our tensions, but feeling worn out nonetheless, we greeted the staff member (who had accompanied Corinne and was in charge of us) with our song of 'I'll Be Around' and all went off to bed.

Shortly after six, after scarcely two hours' sleep, Corinne pounded on our door, awakening us with the electrifying news that the invasion had started. Our first reaction was that this was another of her practical jokes (to which she seemed partial), but then we were ecstatic and also a little miffed at not having been told by our crew since we must have flown over all that activity and missed it all.

We all went back to bed and got up later, when the newspapers were delivered. We read them avidly and listened to the radio without learning much. I remember playing several games of ping-pong with Corinne and Bob while Staunton was obtaining details of why the drop had not taken place. It turned out, as Staunton told us on the way to lunch in another borrowed car, that it was assumed the reception committee had been disturbed by a patrol, but by pre-arrangement should be expecting us tonight.

I cannot explain why, but on the third of our by now almost routine checkouts my morale (and that of the group as well) had reverted to the almost unconcerned level of our first attempt: there was virtually no tension or hesitancy. Perhaps the excitement of the invasion had had some effect. By now the Customs inspector knew us well enough to wave us through after a friendly 'good evening'. This time our plane was a US Air Force Liberator that had come up from Harrington for this flight, its American crew a little more informal than their British predecessors. I had resolved how to carry my box of crystals inside my jumpsuit though it was still held in place by the harness straps. Shortly after takeoff we had asked that the hole be left at least partially open so that we might get to see some of the action going on below, but the request was turned down emphatically by the captain as unsafe and against all known regulations.

The flight was pleasant with considerable banter among us as we played fairly enthusiastic games of twenty-one and gin rummy in the almost total darkness. The time seemed to pass quickly and I was somewhat surprised when the warning light came on, our static lines were hooked up, and the hole uncovered. As we sat around waiting with our feet on the edge of the open hole, Staunton was looking up at the light with, I thought, a rather exaggerated concentrated nonchalance. Bob, with a similar nonchalance, and perhaps a little theatricality, was stifling a yawn. I don't really remember doing anything to hide my tenseness other than smiling at Corinne, who had winked, and looking down at the ground, which was lit by a brighter moon than on the previous night. It seemed more wooded than open and I had a fleeting image of being hung up in a tree. We made a second pass and the dispatcher gestured us away from the hole. Dismayed, we had just eased away from the hole and were starting to unhook our static lines when the warning light came on again. We felt the engines throttling back and a mad repositioning around the hole took place almost concurrently with the issuance of the order 'action stations'. Staunton and Corinne were facing one another across the hole with their backs to the sides of the plane while Bob and I were opposite each other on the other axis. We scarcely had time to get perched with our feet ready to swing into the hole and our hands on the edge ready to push off before the GO command was uttered. Staunton went first and as his shoulders and head disappeared I saw Corinne disappear before I automatically swung around, pushed up, and followed her into the darkness, eyes shut and probably gritting my teeth. Bob was last.

I felt the 'chute snap open, looked around briefly for some reference point or Staunton, saw neither and hit the ground. There had been no sensation of floating, the descent had seemed very brief, but the landing (while unexpected) had not been hard. I had seen no other 'chutes and noted nothing during the short seven-hundred-foot drop. I landed quite close to some trees apparently at one end or side of the drop zone. I was conscious of the airplane's engine noise somewhere in the near distance as I got out of my harness and unzipped my jumpsuit before folding up my 'chute. I took out my box of crystals to lay them aside before I bent over to work on the 'chute and to my horror I felt the crystals cascade out of one end of the box, which had been torn open. The action of removing the box from the suit had provided a certain momentum which distributed the crystals over a rather wide area. I kneeled with sudden panic in the thick, damp grass feeling for the twelve little two-inch squares, half an inch thick with two prongs at one end that were our means of contact with England and my responsibility.

Frantically combing through the grass, I had found more than half of them and had just begun picking up another few I had finally located when I heard voices. As I hurriedly finished stuffing these last crystals back into the box, I looked up and saw the *képi* of a *gendarme* rising from behind some bushes topping a slight depression not far away, his head and shoulders appearing in turn as he approached. His head was turned away from me as he loudly and emphatically stated, 'I'm certain I saw one of them come down over here.' I had never been told about nor anticipated that any *gendarmes* might be in the reception committee and was very alarmed, not to mention frightened. I don't know what I expected to accomplish (something juvenile and heroic no doubt) as I drew my pistol and cocked it. Just then Staunton's head appeared right behind the *gendarme*. I made my presence known and explained my crystals situation to Staunton, who took it calmly since I was only missing one frequency and he was concerned about Bob, who was not yet accounted for. Meanwhile, the *gendarme* efficiently picked up my 'chute. As we all made our way to the other side of the drop zone, where Bob eventually joined us (having landed at the far end), I learned that Staunton had landed very close to the reception committee and that apparently we had been dropped along the edge of the length of the drop zone. This was partially the fault of the reception committee, who had placed their identification light somewhat near the center of the zone and to one side near woods, which afforded them cover if needed.

There was a brief, enthusiastic welcome by the reception committee before we were bundled into a police car and driven safely and in style to the village of Sussac, a few kilometers away. It was only later that we learned that the police had joined the *maquis* that very night and had been logically assigned to transport us, with no thought as to how we might react to finding them there unexpectedly. Still euphoric, we stopped on a corner of the village square, were ushered through the small, rather bare local store providing a combination of groceries and hardware into a large, well-lit kitchen in the back. There we were greeted by another small group, among whom was a small, mild man introduced as Commandant Charles, who claimed to have a ranking authority in whatever organization existed. The sincerity and warmth, and indeed the near reverence of their greetings was touching, gratifying, and quite surprising, as was their simple acceptance that four individuals speaking perfect French could be British, Canadian, and American. In no time corks popped as wine bottles were opened and eager questions asked by both parties. The invasion was toasted several times, they were awed by our dropping in by parachute, wanted details; we wanted to know the local situation under the occupation. One of the women thought, quite rightly, that we must be hungry, and before she could say what she had to offer, we almost as one asked for eggs. The first and strong reaction was that eggs were unworthy, inappropriate, and certainly insufficient for such an occasion, but they quickly served us beautiful eggs sunny side up when we explained that we hadn't eaten fresh eggs in over a year, being limited to powdered ones (which they had never heard of and could scarcely believe existed). They made faces of disapproval at the very thought.

Those eggs, with fresh bread and butter, were one of the high spots of the evening for me. Finally, sometime after 2 a.m., the greetings ended. Bob and I were given a room with a big double bed, and exhausted and quite relaxed from the wine, I immediately went to sleep without even realizing that Bob was still up. It wasn't until the next morning, fully aware of the coarseness of the linen sheets, which were undoubtedly a part of the housewife's original trousseau, that I felt as if I had really come home to France, for it reminded me a little of my eighty-year-old Tante Katrinette who, when we stayed overnight at her farm, always gave us her best, least used linen sheets from her huge original trousseau. She had hand-embroidered them during her youth before her marriage, but unfortunately they were still almost coarse enough to scratch.

We were awakened about nine the next morning with a small tumbler of calvados, an apple liquor I always had thought of as being only from Normandy. Staunton and Corinne were just starting breakfast (eggs, of course) when I joined them. Others in the room were enjoying some of the little real coffee we had brought. Our suitcases and the radio set had been brought in. Staunton and I coded a brief message announcing our safe arrival and, with Commandant Charles, the five of us set off to make my first operational transmission. Fortunately, the schedule did not call for the frequency of the one lost crystal.

We settled on an isolated spot on a hill off a dirt road, mostly because the scheduled time caught us there. It was completely unconcealed and vulnerable. As I threw a rock attached to the end of my antenna over the single wire that ran from the telegraph pole in front of which we had stopped (the only elevation around), Staunton worried that it might cause complications on the first contact, with which he also hoped to impress Commandant Charles. I did not know if it would or not, but went ahead with outward confidence since I had no other choice. With four people watching me as I tuned the set crouching uncomfortably on the ground, I was nervous and getting more tense as I sent my unanswered call letters out for the third time. To my enormous relief the Home Station came back loud and clear, receipted my message, and I was off the air within the brief time training had emphasized. Commandant Charles was suitably impressed, I suppose, and the rest of us assured that we had contact with London. The operation had officially begun. I adjusted my watch for I had realized that in my anxiousness to perform well I had started my contact a little early.

Two days later, by the ninth of June (thanks to Staunton's and Commandant Charles' efforts), I was settled into a tiny, abandoned house screened by hedges and trees from the dirt road that led to an old water mill about a kilometer from the village. I spent a whole day cleaning it and getting it habitable. It comprised a single large room with a door and a window and a single light bulb hanging from the center of the ceiling. At times the light bulb was visibly pulsing from its hesitant, local sixty-cycle source. In addition, there were two alcoves, a small one with a pump and a stone slab as a sink (which drained out into a hedge outside), and the other one with a window. The outhouse was hidden not far away in the bushes. Two bedsteads with somewhat sagging springs and dubious mattresses had appeared from somewhere along with pillows and blankets, followed (at my request) by a table and two chairs. Staunton had planned to stay there with me and, indeed, did spend much time there early on, but as our activities expanded he scarcely ever really resided there though I was in virtually daily contact with him, either in person or through someone else. In point of fact, Staunton spent few nights there, though he was there for many long evenings and early morning sessions.

It was indeed my own place. The second bed was placed in the large room with the table and chairs which served as my bedroom and work area. The small grocery store of our first night fortunately carried double sockets which allowed me to screw in both a light bulb and have an outlet for the radio. Only about a week later did I get around to finding a small hotplate, some dishes, silver, pots and pans. In the meantime, I ate all my meals in a local café and, more often than not, continued to do so mostly due to time limitations, the very little cooking I did at home involved coffee (roasted barley), herbal tea (linden flowers), and eggs with fresh bread from the bakery, usually the light white bread with local wheat, not the darker kind that most of the rest of the country had.

The second evening in France, Corinne and I left the restaurant to take a stroll to show her where I was located, she pushing an old but serviceable bicycle. We had set out exploring the village environs going down a long hill, and we bummed a ride for the uphill return on the back of a horse-drawn cart, which luckily was headed toward the mill. It was the first time we had been alone together since we had met. We had a pleasant, relaxing stroll and ride, talking easily about developments since our arrival, her very high opinion of Staunton and her complete agreement with his outlook that one has to take chances in life, and that indeed life itself can be defined as a chance. There was no bravado in her expression of that philosophy, only a rather calm conviction. (In retrospect, I have thought that her words were for my benefit.) Other than mentioning that she was going to do some traveling the day after, she revealed nothing about herself and I asked for none. She left as soon as she had seen my location as it was almost dark when we had arrived. I had high hopes that I would have many occasions to spend time together for I was quite taken with her. I happily set to work encoding a long message from Staunton and got ready to listen to Broadcast.

The Broadcast existed to reduce the dangerous Field Station to Home Station transmission time by handling all non-critical traffic from the Home Station with no transmissions or receipt required by the Field Station until the next field transmission. It occurred twice daily: verbally after the regular daily BBC French news broadcast in the early evening, and in a Morse code transmission starting around 9 p.m. The BBC news program often ended with rather senseless sentences or phrases purporting to be messages to friends and family from Frenchmen in England. These sometimes represented the reading of a phrase provided for someone who required guarantee of good faith from an agent in France, but in our case, as in most others, ours announced a forthcoming drop at the drop zone identified by the phrase. I still remember the first such message I heard on Broadcast, was obviously struck by it, and still wonder whose it might have been: 'Joséphine a des fesses d'ébène' (Josephine has ebony buttocks). Many were witty though most were plain and nondescript. If more than one drop was to be made, the statement 'we repeat' and the appropriate number of drops preceded the phrase before it was repeated. For example, 'Remember the great raspberries in mother's garden, we repeat two times, remember the great raspberries in mother's garden' signified that two drops on that DZ (drop zone) were to occur the following night, each drop being a planeload. Initially, my responsibility for the BBC news was only to make sure that Staunton had heard it, but the primary task was to listen to the Broadcast in Morse code around 9 p.m. and copy and decode the messages. I was one of four recipients in the particular Broadcast cycle to which I was assigned, and I was the third in the order of receipt. At the start of the Broadcast it was blessedly indicated who had how many messages, which did not eliminate the tedious task of listening to the meaningless transmissions intended for the recipients who preceded me if I had messages, but did leave me free if I had none. However, if there was even one, even very short, it could easily be well into the night by the time I received and decoded it.

This was the beginning of what quickly became my very busy routine existence without much regular sleep. In addition to the coding and decoding (which consumed a great deal of time even though I developed a thorough working familiarity with the letters that would result from the double transposition exercise), every day I had one formally scheduled period that varied randomly over the twenty-four-hour period in which to send any traffic, which at this time was heavy indeed. If I had nothing to send, I still was expected to listen in case Home Station was trying to make contact. The scheduled time varied day to day, as did its call signs and the pre-established frequency for the transmission. There were also several alternative schedules each day. These could be used for emergency contacts, but were normally used when the original schedule frequency was unusable due to static or other difficult conditions, or if the length or number of messages allowed too much time for enemy detection, the change thus forcing the latter to locate the sender again.

To make it even more difficult for the enemy, and primarily to eliminate an unhealthy dependency on local power, within a few weeks I managed to obtain two twelve-volt car batteries, despite their scarcity and at considerable expense and difficulty, so that if power were cut during my transmissions (which occurred more often than one liked, either due to normal power failure or to enemy detection attempts), the area from which my radio was operating could not be identified except through direction finding. Our rural area was relatively free of German movement and most reports of slow-moving vans in the area, though very infrequent, did not seem to be applicable to me. I was perhaps a little jittery as a result of quite frequent overflights by a small plane which I noticed within a week of our arrival. Once or twice it even seemed to circle. In retrospect, it may have been simply a courier, but I saw no reason to take chances. However, the batteries had to be recharged.

In response to my request to London for some means of recharging these batteries, a reception committee one morning brought me a box identified as a steam generator. Inside was a beautiful little steam engine with shiny brass and painted a beautiful green color. It looked like what it indeed was, an expensive toy to which was attached a small generator. I immediately took it out into the yard, filled it with water, lit a fire of small twigs in its miniscule firebox and, feeling a little foolish, spent the next hours listening to it chug away, constantly replenishing the water and feeding the fire. The results were more than disappointing. It did charge the batteries, but at such a slow rate that it would have taken several days of constantly refilling the tiny boiler and minding the fire. Such an expenditure of time was entirely unacceptable, and some local happily took the engine (less the generating apparatus). Fortunately, I found a local electrician, a close friend of the water mill's owner, and together we devised a way to utilize the water mill's wheel to generate a steady charge through a Rube Goldberg set of straps, belts, and assorted wheels which increased the gentle turn of the water wheel to a speed sufficient to power a small generator that had been obtained somewhere, somehow. I now felt liberated from dependence on local power; double transposition coding assured us a degree of security; and we were all incognito on the air. We were referred to only by code names in the messages. Staunton was 'Hamlet', I was 'Virgile', Corinne was 'Seamstress', and Bob was 'Porter'.

'Salesman' was the name of the operation under Staunton's direction. I learned this only at the end of the operation. It was also, as I much later discovered, the name of his previous operation in the Rouen area. I don't recall having been briefed before my departure, other than in rather general terms about the mission. My cover story and the French clothing issued to me had led me to envision a mission in a city or town. As it turned out, I feel we could just as well have jumped in uniform for, as I very soon discovered, we were to organize, unify, arm, train, and direct the operations of the many local resistance groups or *maquis* in our area. '*Maquis*' was a Corsican term adopted by the French for the scrub brush into which men went into hiding when pursued by the law. These *maquis* had grown in numbers when in early 1943 the German and Vichy police began sweeping up men between the ages of twenty and thirty-five for service in Germany or Russia. London wisely began doing its best to sustain such groups seeking to escape that fate with false ration cards, clothing, and some weapons, and as they multiplied, it became more and more obvious that with training and considerable direction, these many small groups could be very effective and would be more likely to survive than larger, more organized units. These groups, in fact, supplanted the original concept of a large *armée secrète* that would be available when needed, and the validity of the decision was proven after the Vercors debacle in 1943.

Yet before D-Day, the *maquis* had also often been the refuge of petty criminals as well as men at risk with the authorities for some reason, personal or political, rather than an expression of any great patriotism. The accusation that *maquisards* were nothing better than bandits had in too many instances some validity, especially in the very early stages, when the men had to sustain themselves as best they could without any outside support to speak of in a local ambience of intolerance since any activity on their part, indeed their very presence, was often cause for German retribution on the population.

The groups varied in political outlook as well as social makeup, and tended to differ quite significantly in outlook from the then not very numerous other small resistance groups in that they were not for the most part comprised of motivated, regularly employed people, living at home, who at much risk mounted what operations they could around their daily lives. They were living on the fringes of society and often just managing to survive in the woods. However, both groups as often as not could and did work together.

Staunton's shortly-before-departure London briefing had, it seems, not mentioned that the various *maquis* we were to utilize effectively (starting with the one we dropped into) were not only groups that were very disorganized, independent, and individualistic, but also often strongly conflicting ones politically. As he stated in his first report: 'I have been given to understand that I would find on arrival a very well-organized *maquis*, strictly devoid of any political intrigues, which would constitute a very good basis for extending the circuit throughout the area.' Instead, as he and I encoded, though there was indeed a *maquis* here, it was very much an untrained *maquis* and commanded by the most completely incompetent people he had ever dealt with. Indeed, their performance to date seemed to have been negligible and it took Staunton hours of discussions to get even a small operation organized and agreed to. Fortunately, by 9 June he had made contact with another small, local group that was more than willing to take direction. It was this group ('Bistro', I think) that was the first we equipped, trained, and used while still trying to instill some organization into the one we had dropped into.

Yet all these *maquis* had much going for them. The immediate locale of the Haute Vienne department, an area with many small farming villages and much wild country, mountainous and wooded, was perfect for guerrillas in terms of terrain and food supplies. Limoges, the major industrial city in the area, was under the complete, tight control of the Germans, who had developed it into their command center for the region. However, the primary importance of the region at this time, for us, lay in the fact that the main roads and rail lines north from both Toulouse and Bordeaux ran through it. Our immediate primary mission was to utilize these *maquis* to delay German reinforcements moving to Normandy from the south. We were receiving reports that advanced detachments of the SS Panzer Division *Das Reich* were already starting to move up from Toulouse though, in fact, the bulk of the division inexplicably remained around Toulouse several weeks after D-Day.

To hope to accomplish this objective with any success, Staunton needed a much larger force. Some twenty *gendarmes* had joined the first of our associated *maquis* (Bistro) immediately after D-Day, while remaining on official duty; they were indeed a most welcome disciplined addition. Some of their earliest members were on our reception committee. Staunton had established contact with that *maquis* group within two days of our arrival and, while a start, he still needed to contact, coordinate, and direct as many of the activities of the neighboring *maquis* as possible in the Corrèze, Creuse, Charente, and Indre departments through which the Germans would also be moving. These were all operating independently, and he knew relatively little of their strength and effectiveness, or even exactly where they were. There was still a certain degree of the defeatism and apathy that pervaded after the 1940 defeat, though there were many anti-Pétain patriots also. In our region it was primarily the extremist factions of the right and the left, the pro-Pétain *milice* and the anti-Pétain communists respectively, who seemed to have been most motivated and active initially, while the Pétain government represented a certain stability and even normalcy to a large portion of the general population. So Staunton had to determine the extent of their willingness to cooperate. With the invasion many more men would be motivated to join the *maquis* and there was no doubt that they would welcome the supplies we could provide, though this did not necessarily assure their proper use or the acceptance of our direction.

The first step toward the creation of any such effective, coordinated force was taken on 10 June, three days after our arrival. Corinne was sent to make contact with other *maquis* leaders. I didn't know her initial destination or contact, but I was familiar through my transmissions with Nestor, Faure, Samuel, and Hector, *maquis* leaders who were our 'neighbors', and I assumed she was to get in touch with them and let them know we were ready to help them and coordinate our efforts. It turned out that it was in fact Samuel, 160 kilometers to the southwest of us, whom she was to contact.

I was very busily engaged in coding and sending a few first descriptions and coordinates for some prospective drop zones (DZ) for approval as well as first requests for specific supplies. I had been specifically and purposely divorced from any personal involvement with all the military aspects of the operation by Staunton, beginning with my first transmission at the start of the operation (much to my chagrin and disappointment), necessary to safeguard his critical link of communication with London. I was to remain in my civilian clothes, a mysterious person not known to many. Initially, I had little direct knowledge of the daily activities around me other than through the traffic I handled. So it was not until a day later that I was made aware of the terrible news when Staunton came in around mid-afternoon and asked when was the earliest we could contact

London. He then told me the news that Corinne had been captured after a long running fight; she had tried to make it to the relative safety of a nearby wood. The person who had been with her (code name 'Anastasie') was also thought to have been taken. Corinne was reported to have been seen being taken into the prison in Limoges.

There was a flurry of traffic during which I developed a great deal of admiration for all the Base Station operators' expertise, as the static was terrible, requiring much repetition and several changes of frequency. The depressing shock of the news was, for me at least, somewhat ameliorated by Staunton's clear, calm, and practical positive thinking. I believe now that he may have done it in part for my benefit, to keep up my morale, for I cannot see how he could have been that hopeful in the situation he was facing. As I found out later, they had been together on a previous mission and worked closely and very successfully as a team. The only negative thought I can remember him expressing was blaming himself for not having forbidden Corinne to go by car and not having insisted that she use her bike. He also initially did express some condemnation of the man who had accompanied her for his lack of judgement and devil-may-care attitude.

Two days later, on 13 June, Anastasie returned. He had managed to escape capture. He provided confirmation to the information Staunton had already been collecting from people at the site of the incident, as well as many more details on what had happened. Initially, there was some condemnation of his conduct, his seemingly having abandoned Corinne, and even of his three-day delay in reporting back. I certainly felt that way, almost certainly based on prejudice since I didn't know him then. It turned out that this criticism was in most respects unfounded. In the next few days further contact with a Limoges resistance group (which had reported the news of her imprisonment in that city's prison) now told us that a contact had been made with one of her jailers, who agreed to report on what was happening to her and requested money to 'help look after her'. Certain expenses that he requested were paid over a period of about two or three weeks. In exchange, we received the information that she was as well as could be expected.

We had been told she was limping badly and was being interrogated by the Gestapo. In the following days I was aware that plans were being made to try to rescue her. We learned that she was being escorted to Gestapo headquarters on foot by only two soldiers from the prison for daily interrogation. Plans to attack the soldiers, get Corinne into a car and out of Limoges through a roadblock that had been overcome were prepared by Bob, but they were never carried out: she was transferred north, presumably to Paris, before the plans could be implemented and she disappeared. When Limoges was liberated we discovered that she had been there only a few days, we had been led on by a rapacious jailer. I was told he had been 'taken care of' by some of the rough justice courts then operating.

It was almost four months later, at the end of the operation, that I found out more of what exactly had occurred and, incidentally, Corinne's real name (Violette Szabó). Anastasie (Jacques Dufour) was an active leader in our *maquis* and knew some of the people Corinne was to contact. He had volunteered to introduce her to them to provide a bona fides, starting with one south of Arnac-Pompadour (the town from which Mme de Pompadour, the mistress of Louis XV, took her name). She would in turn then be put in contact with other groups, making those contacts by bike. However, instead of going to the first meeting by bike (a normal, unsuspicious mode of travel), he urged her to go by car. It would be easier, quicker, and he knew the area well. He said it was only some fifty kilometers (actually it was twice that distance) and reassured Staunton that he would be back the same day, since he was needed on hand to work with our local *maquis* operations. Staunton must have agreed to the use of the car for expediency's sake, there being so many contacts to make, but he made certain they were armed because they would not be able to talk their way out of a checkpoint situation, which this mode of transportation was likely to entail. He gave Corinne a Sten gun with a couple of extra magazines and Anastasie had a Marlin submachine gun.

I don't know whether Staunton was aware at that time that Anastasie was wanted (under his real name) by the Germans and the *milice* (the Pétain regime's Gestapo), or that he had agreed to stop at the small village of La Croisille to pick up a friend called Jean Bariaud, who was to accompany him on his return trip after Corinne had arrived at her destination. Corinne's bicycle was tied to the side of the car.

They would have had to cross Route Nationale 20, one of the main highways from the south, to get to their destination in Corrèze. Anastasie apparently planned to cross it at Salon-la-Tour, his home village, which was just off that main road. It was just as they were approaching Salon-la-Tour that they spotted a checkpoint manned by Germans some fifty yards from a T-intersection just outside the village. There was no question of bluffing their way through. They all got out of the car. Bariaud, being unarmed, immediately ran (eventually getting back to La Croisille with the first report of the roadblock incident), while Anastasie and Corinne ran crouching along a ditch and over a fence into a farmyard under the German fire that had started as soon as they had stepped out of the car armed. From there they passed through a neighboring farmyard, past a hedge, across a meadow and the stream at its lower end. They gained a little lead when the farmer in the second farm misdirected the Germans, but they were soon spotted running up through a corn field toward a dirt road that crossed the railroad tracks by a small overpass at the top of the rise and some woods. The constant fire from their pursuers, the tiring zigzagging, and covering each other as they ran was more than Corinne could manage. She could go no further.

As we found out much later, she had been slightly wounded in one arm and it is possible that the ankle she had hurt in a previous jump school session had given out. Some 400 meters from the potential safety of the woods, she could go no further, but insisted that Anastasie escape as he was more important to the *maquis*. She kept on firing, covering his escape until she ran out of ammunition and was captured. There were two versions of what happened and they varied depending on the teller. Anastasie had continued to run up towards the road on which the armored cars were approaching. He got there with just enough time to hide under a small haystack or a loosely stacked pile of logs near another farmyard with the help of the farmer's daughters, whom he knew well.

To this day, I have no idea which is the correct version, though I feel Staunton's version of the haystack is more likely. After the Germans had finished searching the area and left, Anastasie stayed in hiding with the farmer's family for two days. He was with them that first evening when Staunton was making inquiries in the area seeking information on what had happened after being notified through Bariaud.

The checkpoint had been manned by advance elements of the SS Panzer Division *Das Reich* trying to counter *maquis* activity in the area, both in preparation for movement of the division through the area and to find out who had captured some of their men and one of their officers. These same advance groups massacred the inhabitants of Oradour-sur-Glane, burning the village to the ground with its inhabitants locked inside buildings and machine-gunning all who tried to escape. The tragic irony is that it was the wrong target. The SS thought they were teaching a lesson to the village of Oradour-sur-Vayres.

In spite of the terrible shock of that event so early in our operation, we were too busy to mourn Corinne's capture and disappearance for long. She was not forgotten, just completely out of our reach. New drop zones were being surveyed, described, and approved and, more importantly, beginning to be used. New groups were being contacted and incorporated under our guidance and direction; those of Bernard around Pressac, of Huart around Gramont and Blond. The units were politically varied, some AS (Armée Secrète), some FTP (Francs Tireurs Partisans), and others heavily communist. Almost all had a certain distrust of one another. Staunton immediately and firmly began working to eliminate that distrust and formed these units into a cohesive whole. This was not an easy task. While the organizing and training was being initiated, Staunton was still having trouble getting control of our base *maquis* operations.

To complicate matters, it seemed that there were two Commandant Charleses. There was the local one we knew, who was more and more unable, or unwilling, to approve or move on our selected targets. There was also a shadowy second Commandant Charles (a former saxophone player with ambition and good intentions) who, in spite of gross incompetence, had managed somehow to come from the Châteauroux area and be accepted as a coordinator of neighboring *maquis* groups. However, he was unable to provide any sort of real leadership, control, direction, supplies, or any semblance of coordinated operational decisions.

It turned out that this second Commandant Charles was merely a fiction to cover for our local Commandant Charles. His claim to fame (we later discovered) had been to deceive London into dropping supplies into the region after making radio contacts through another group and inventively identifying and promoting 'the well-organized *maquis*' to which we had been assigned. There was indeed a *maquis* but it was not under his direction. We had no knowledge of this situation at the time.

It very soon became apparent that our Commandant Charles was really a figurehead. To gain control and make certain that something would be accomplished, Staunton finally drew a line; Charles would do as he was ordered or there would be no supplies. Ensuing discussions led Staunton, Bob, and I to feel somewhat threatened. There was even some probably ill-founded fear that I might be taken hostage, which could have broken communications with London and would have also adversely affected any other operational developments for our group with the other *maquis* we were in the process of contacting and training. It was a very tense period as frequent and unrewarding discussions continued until we discovered that the real power in the area was one Georges Guingoin, a former corporal and self-appointed colonel.

Georges Guingoin was a tall man with a full head of black hair, always clean shaven, his eyes somewhat hidden by the very thick lenses of his glasses. He spoke with a pronounced southern accent. He usually wore civilian clothes that (with his very flat feet) contradicted his claim of military rank. He had been a poorly paid schoolteacher in Saint-Gilles, taken prisoner in the debacle of 1940, escaped and decided to resist. A hardline communist, he slowly built up the local resistance. In his favor was the fact that Russia and Germany were still allies, and as a result, the Vichy police didn't harass him. That changed when Hitler invaded Russia. Guingoin was the head of the Communist party in the region and had been (I believe) a communist deputy for the Haute Vienne. He apparently felt that we 'Allied forces' that had reached him might be a threat to his movement when the war was over.

During all the following discussions, which were now conducted directly with Guingoin, we continued operations, primarily using the newly contacted 'Bistro' group as our primary forces, with which we continued the stoppage of rail traffic north, sometimes with spectacular success (the blockage of the Salon-la-Tour cut). It became apparent that our base Haute Vienne *maquis* was not only very ineffective without our support, but also that Guingoin's prestige as the initiator of resistance in the region was being adversely affected.

All the while, Staunton continued discussions with him, stressing that we were only interested in winning the war, and that local politics did not interest us. It would be much more to Guingoin's advantage to cooperate fully with the Allies, as were the Russians, thereby increasing his prestige and consolidating his position of power. Facing shortages of supplies, the reality that much was being accomplished without him, a small growing discontent among his own men, and feeling pressure from other groups, he finally accepted our sincerity, and thereafter cooperated fully, stressing to his great advantage 'our active participation under his leadership' in a pamphlet post-liberation of Limoges. Things were settled before late June, and while he did not yet accept the FFI (Forces Françaises de l'Intérieure) politically, his operations were directed, probably unknown to him, through Staunton by SOE and General Koenig of the FFI under de Gaulle in London.

During this very early phase of the operation, Bob (our only explosives expert) was out virtually every night blowing up tracks and derailing trains. As soon as others had received their hands-on training, they were sent out on their own. The success rate was good, with nightly disruptions of the northbound rails throughout the area most accessible to us, encompassing Brive, Tulle, and Uzerche. There were a few exceptions to the regular success such as when, having placed the charges and camouflaged everything, no one thought to check a switch and, to the dismay and mockery of all, the train sailed past on another track. It was stopped further up the line by a somewhat 'independent' operation that we couldn't really condemn.

But in addition to the routine traffic interruptions, which were usually repaired within two days, Staunton led a group that completely blocked traffic for two months in late June by wrecking two trains in the deep cut just south of Salon-la-Tour. The heavy equipment required to clear the wreckage was not available immediately, and during that time we mounted constant attacks on all the alternative routes so that virtually nothing got through. We capped that session by destroying the repair cranes, of which there were few, with the result that the two-day average repair time was considerably extended. The bridge at Saint-Germain and two others around Pierre-Buffière were also demolished. In point of fact, throughout June and July, the Bordeaux and Toulouse mainline traffic north to Limoges and Paris was slowed to an insignificant, unreliable trickle. High-tension power lines were destroyed too, cutting off the electricity supply for the submarine base at Rochefort.

We were not quite so successful with the road traffic, however, especially on the main roads, which were used more and more as the summer progressed and the railroads became less reliable. Convoys still got through our constant ambushes, but never unscathed. Though I was supposed to limit my activities to maintaining communications, I did manage to participate in several of our early ambushes in 'not dangerous' positions. To my surprise, the traffic was not all trucks; it was astounding how much the German army still relied on horse-drawn vehicles.

Our main weapons in ambushes were Sten guns (slow rate of fire and short range) and the Gammon grenade, whose explosive charge (even when not supplemented with odds and ends for shrapnel) was most effective in stunning and stopping vehicles. The German troops always reacted swiftly, effectively, and forcefully to all ambushes, and we seldom accomplished any significant halt in the traffic or inflicted serious damage, though we did cause considerable delays and forced them to take many detours and use the more confusing and less direct secondary roads. While the degree of destruction was limited, it did initially achieve the primary objective of causing long delays, annoyance, and having some impact on morale.

By mid-July the attacks, which had mostly been small, involving only grenades and light weapons, had grown to a somewhat larger scale, complete with roadblocks and bazookas, to even more unorthodox attacks such as those performed by a group of Spaniards (Republican refugees from the civil war). They had suffered greatly in the conflict, hoped for little other than revenge, were anti-fascist in the extreme, and reckless. On several occasions they attacked German convoys laboring up a long hill by driving toward them in a Citroën with the roof cut open. Some stood up, firing automatic weapons and tossing Gammon grenades (a detonator device whose safety pin was attached to a short ribbon with a lead weight at the end that unwound, pulling the pin as it flew through the air and went off on impact, and to which was attached a skirt of material holding up to two pounds of plastic explosives and anything else one cared to add) while others blazed away through the side and rear windows as they drove down the whole length of the convoy. For reasons unexplained no German vehicle ever turned out into their lane, which would have been the end of that operation.

My participation in all of this activity was rather limited. I had had only cursory training in drop zone (DZ) operations, for receiving drops at night, but, in part to keep me happy and partly because he needed coordination and I could be very helpful in this area, Staunton relaxed the restriction against me participating in dangerous activities. I was thus involved as often as radio work permitted with the activities of the reception committees, mostly ones relatively near my base, which allowed my participation even when I had Broadcast (provided it had been a relatively brief session). Since the planes normally arrived around 11 p.m., I could usually make sure the team was assembled if the DZ was not too far from my radio, catch the Broadcast, return in time for the drop and complete any decoding after the drop was over. When returning after Broadcast, I could also check that the DZ was clear, for we were sometimes delayed or interrupted by roaming patrols.

Reception committee work was not particularly exciting since it involved a great deal of waiting, but it was thoroughly enjoyable during a quiet, moonlit summer night. The peacefulness supplanted the constant possibility of being interrupted. This, of course, changed to anticipation and excitement when the first soft, distant drone of the airplane was heard. As it came closer, the recognition signal (the Morse code letter assigned to the drop zone) was flashed at where the plane was thought to be since they never showed any lights. We never had an S-phone with which we could have spoken directly to the plane nor even the Eureka, which would have provided a beam that the pilot could follow to the DZ. It was often a hit and miss affair. Sometimes the plane had to circle to come at the DZ in the right direction or, to our great disappointment, the pilot failed to see the recognition signal, or it was not for us and kept going. But if it was for us, the drone became louder until it finally came in low with a roar and the swish of disturbed air, and the containers dropped out and quickly floated down as the sound of the plane started to fade or it turned to make another pass.

Then the real work began. Summer nights were short and the moon our primary source of light for locating and collecting all the containers before daylight. They were not always very accurately dropped, landing (indeed too often) hundreds of yards, even kilometers away from the DZ or in nearby trees. In our drop, a bundle containing several hundred thousand francs landed right in the courtyard of the local police station. The money was lost to us only temporarily and may have created a problem for the British, but if ever proof were needed of the existence of our clandestine activity, nothing more specific could have been provided. While, generally speaking, our DZs were seldom bothered, there were enough instances of forced cancellation. Other interference caused by the proximity of German or pro-Vichy forces, or being required to show ID papers when returning home at dawn claiming to be on the way to work, was relatively rare.

By far the most important duty was keeping count of the containers, up to a dozen per drop, each a circular tube about thirty inches in diameter, about six feet long, and weighing some 150–200 pounds. Some could be broken down into three sections, which facilitated moving them, but the whole exercise took a well-coordinated effort, especially since it was done in the dark, had to be done quietly and with minimum traces of any activity left behind. The reception committees I dealt with usually included some of the *gendarmes* who had joined us after D-Day, and their reliability in collecting, and especially delivering to us, everything that had been dropped, was critical. I usually left right after the plane had made its final pass if I had decoding to do. To this day, whenever I happen to hear the ever-more rare sound of a propeller-driven plane at night that whole ambience of DZ activity returns vividly.

I also occasionally participated in DZ site selection. It was during such a job that I had to show my false papers for the first time. That first occurrence (in retrospect, an unnecessarily tense one for me) involved scouting for a possible DZ quite far from our normal operating zone. I had just left my bike at the edge of the field and penetrated a small wood that screened it from the road, and was about to start my evaluation when a patrol in a small truck appeared and drew up to my bike. I had heard them coming, realized that I could not hide, and by the time they had stopped I had come back out onto the road buttoning my pants (perhaps a little too ostentatiously) as though I had just relieved myself. I suppose I was lucky that the patrol was not French, for they would no doubt have been suspicious of any Frenchman moving into bushes to relieve himself when the edge of the road offered a perfectly acceptable place.

This patrol was non-German, though in German uniforms, from one of many conquered countries providing troops and goods to the Reich. The noncom in charge spoke a little French, and I had no trouble explaining my presence in the middle of nowhere with a Michelin road map in hand (thankfully still unmarked) by claiming to be searching for a particular farm where I had been told I could obtain eggs, meat, and butter. They, too, were apparently more engaged in foraging for food than in monitoring and controlling the local area, for this information aroused their interest far more than who I was or what I was about. This also created a complication since I had to convince the noncom that I did not know where this farm was and that I was not keeping information from him. Though tense and nervous initially, it quickly became perfectly normal to lie and dissemble with ease and conviction. A certain calm and, indeed, normalcy took over, even to the point of showing them the map and asking for their opinion as to where I was and where this farm might be. To be sure, this was a routine situation (almost a break in their boredom), and I am certain they were every bit as interested in the food as I made believe I was. They passed on, wishing me luck and suggesting, not just in jest, that I bring something back for them, to which I appeared to acquiesce. Needless to say, I went home another way when I had finished my evaluation. My quite limited experience with checkpoints (after that first nervous one) led me to conclude that they were normally routine and searching not for anything specific but on the lookout for anything out of the ordinary; nevertheless, I knew quite well that on occasion they were also set up for very specific purposes.

It was also in these early stages that I very occasionally (when not tied up with coding or transmissions) had the chance to go to one of the groups' encampments and spend a short time helping Bob and others he had trained as instructors to familiarize the men with the newly received weapons and explosives. I even helped remove cosmoline, the sticky grease the weapons were covered in to preserve them; they were obviously being dropped to us directly from some warehouse. It was a very trying experience to get the stuff off with soap and water instead of gasoline. Though unfamiliar at first with the French names of most of the weapons' components, I could still assist by helping to show how to disassemble, clean, and reassemble them. While my expertise with explosives was not as great as Bob's,

I could help supervise the trainees in handling the TNT, plastics, primacord, blasting caps, fuses, fog signals, and other demolition paraphernalia. It was at least some association with the activist part of the mission.

The men were now beginning to be organized into specific units under a fairly well-organized chain of command, and they were being equipped as quickly as possible with weapons and clothing. There was much sharing of equipment during training sessions. It became ominously apparent that if there was to be growth and cohesion, we had to provide more materiel. Much of my traffic dealt with material requirements and DZ availability and usage. With the cooperation of Guingoin assured, we needed material quickly to consolidate and strengthen our growing regional involvement.

The needs of this whole process of forming a cohesive, effective *maquis*, as well as those of our constant operations, were temporarily resolved when shortly before 25 June (if I remember the date correctly), the late-night coded broadcast alerted us to expect a large drop soon, stressing that it was to be a daylight drop. To have a drop in daylight was novelty enough and to receive a large one that might end some of our shortages and sustain our growth was a major event. Exuberance everywhere! To facilitate moving the anticipated material, we chose a drop zone close to the center of the area, a big open field on top of a plateau (*le borderie*) near Domps, from which distribution to all associated *maquis* could be accomplished more easily.

A subsequent broadcast told us we should be ready for the drop on 25 June sometime after 10 a.m. We thought we were prepared for any eventuality, but we were quite taken aback when the BBC news on 24 June was followed by the DZ-identifying message with a 'we repeat seventy-two times.' There was some static and other interference that made clear understanding difficult. There was disagreement among those who had heard the message: some heard *soixante douze* (seventy-two), others only *douze* (twelve), and others were equally convinced they had heard *soixante* (sixty). We had difficulty convincing ourselves that the higher numbers could be correct, the quantity being so improbably great that it must have been misheard, but, having no time to obtain confirmation, obediently called up what we considered a huge reception committee to be on site by 8 a.m. to handle some quantity possibly greater than twelve but probably not seventy-two. Unexpectedly, many, many more appeared to see the show of a daylight drop, word of the event having spread despite all attempts to limit those informed. Everybody wanted to help; confusion reigned until we managed to get the DZ cleared, and even then we had a large ring of spectators around the edges. As it turned out it was very fortunate that they were there, but for the moment it was a very excitable and voluble French crowd. By 9 a.m. we had three very large fires set up and burning in a straight line down the center of the DZ, as had been prescribed by Broadcast, both to identify it and show wind direction. Next to each were more wood and piles of grasses, hay, and greenery of all kinds to throw on the fire and create the smoke that would act as the beacon. We were fortunate to be able to utilize the excess crowd to amass these materials.

I was so accustomed to night drops that, unthinking, I was next to the fire at the head of the line with a flashlight to give the recognition signal letter. I must have been expecting the planes to be the usual Liberators or Lancasters and to have them come in one at a time, in sequence, as they did at night, or in small groups. Shortly after 10 a.m., we heard the distant sound of planes and the fires were converted to smoke pots with the addition of the greenery. It was only in the midst of this activity that I realized the noise was not the normal one I had expected, but a much more powerful drone, one that came from high up and involved many more than one plane. Then we saw them – all seventy-two! They were in tight formations, not at the sub-1,000-foot altitude we were used to, but almost like toys way up in the sky. Not only were they higher than I had ever seen airplanes (at what seemed to be around 5,000 feet) but they were B-17s!

The excitation and noise level on the ground increased greatly at the sighting, then turned to wonder when clouds of parachutes opened and began to drift down. Many of the onlookers then started to surge onto the DZ, but they stopped almost immediately when they realized that some containers (whose static lines had not been attached to anything) were dropping like bombs, bouncing, breaking apart, and shattering as they hit the ground. This completely unexpected crash delivery seemed to involve a great number of containers and to continue for a few very long minutes. In fact, it's likely that no more than five or six dozen came thundering down on us, but they did not come down *en masse*, rather in a scattered pattern, which must have been the result of a partial release from several planes.

One of those containers scattered its sections all around me, with one actually bouncing and breaking open into the fire and very soon, as the 'chutes came floating peacefully down, we had exploding ammunition adding greatly to the excitement and confusion. In this almost surreal ambience, when the mass of containers had almost all drifted down, two P-51 Mustangs made several buzzing passes at the edge of the plateau. We were almost looking down at the pilots. They waved in response to one *maquis* group imbued with the AS military spirit and service discipline, which had stood to attention, presenting arms as the planes flashed by the second time. Then they began the work.

Water appeared from somewhere to help extinguish the fire under the exploding ammunition so that it could be pulled out of the fire. Teams were organized by sectors of the DZ to locate and retrieve the containers for, having been dropped from so high, they had had more time and opportunity to drift, in some cases well outside the DZ, some more than a kilometer away, not to mention those caught in trees. As they were collected and brought to several central collection points during the following days, they were also counted. We had received a staggering 860 containers! Other teams specialized in collecting damaged containers into a single area. Among these we found two that had smashed together at the edge of the DZ. Some small wooden boxes containing blasting caps in one section had broken and somehow the loose caps had embedded themselves in plastic explosives packed in a broken section of the other container into which it had crashed. We were lucky the mess had not exploded. We needed those blasting caps so desperately that, without authorization, that very afternoon I helped pick them gingerly out of the plastic.

The trucks we had arranged to move the new equipment were totally inadequate. They could only take a maximum of six to eight containers at a time and the wait for them to return for another load was frustratingly long. Fortunately, the activity of rounding up all the containers helped fill the delays. Horse-drawn and oxen-drawn farm wagons were put into service to make the deliveries to the nearest camps. However, everyone was so delighted with the morning's activity that the slow removal caused no complaint; after all, we would have time in the following days to gather, store, and issue the supplies. By sunset things seemed well under control; most of the 'chutes had been removed, some of the damaged container sections had been emptied and the contents distributed directly to the camps with the most pressing needs, and the unmoved majority of the drop was left pretty much where it had landed or been collected, but accounted for and marked with its destination. Within less than a week, it had all been distributed or stored.

After the 25 June daylight drop, the organized training and expansion of all operations went forward at a frantic pace. During June through mid-August, we must have grown to a force 3,000 to 4,000 strong, pretty much 'controlling' on a daily basis (or at least being very active) in an area comprising all of the non-urban Haute Vienne (less Limoges), most of the Corrèze, and portions of the Creuse, Dordogne, and even the Charente departments. Within this area, especially in the Haute Vienne and extending, to a lesser extent, into the more distant parts of the other departments, we had an effectively functioning food purchasing, supply, and distribution system and even an independent local phone system connecting the various camps. This total area was divided into three operating regions; the one I was mostly associated with was east and south of Limoges; the second was west and south of the city; and the third was north and west. All regions took direction from Staunton and shared supplies dropped to us through the DZs we established and whose operations we controlled.

It did not take very long for our mass of 25 June supplies to be distributed and consumed. To keep this growing organization and its operations functioning, we received an average of four to eight drops a night in July, which involved handling some 1,600 containers and several dozen other packages: but it was only on moonlit nights that our supplies arrived, which meant some very busy moonlit nights with reception committees. It was still not enough, and we kept requesting more though we were receiving about all we could physically handle. Our operation had expanded and not only with local recruits: around mid-July, several uniformed visitor groups arrived from London (some of whom were old SOE friends and colleagues of Staunton and Bob). In fact, one of them, de Guélis, was the man who had 'recruited' Bob in Algeria. Staunton and Bob had taken to wearing their uniforms almost as soon as we arrived for the protection of sorts that military impunity might provide in case they were caught during operations. In early July, I abandoned my civilian outfit, at Staunton's insistence, as much for the benefit of military immunity if captured as to receive the prestige of Allied military status rather than remaining an unidentified civilian, and availed myself of a set of enlisted man's olive drab from one of the drops. Somewhere we found insignia, a single 2nd Lt.'s bar and one US insignia, but only one of each rather than the two required. It was only by late August that I managed to get properly outfitted, even to a pair of those longed-for jump boots.

In spite of the expansion of personnel and activities, my workload remained pretty much unchanged. The newly parachuted individuals moved to assigned areas and, for the most part, had their own means of keeping in contact with London and neither increased nor decreased my overall operational traffic. Since very early in the operation I had been hounding Staunton for the chance to participate in operations, and he had finally accepted in early July, but only on the condition that I train a qualified, London-approved replacement. By mid-July, I had successfully reduced the volume of work I personally handled, if not that for which I was still responsible. I managed this reduction at first by limiting my work to enciphering/deciphering and scheduled transmissions, with two assistants (soon reduced to one) doing most of the Broadcast receiving, freeing me for more DZ reception work. I was fortunate in very quickly finding a replacement called Bourg, who had ten years' experience in the French Navy and was quite fluent in German, but had not practiced for four years. Bourg was followed quite shortly by my greatest find, André, who had been the radio operator of General Weygand, the Chief of Staff of the French Army when France fell. After a brief crash training in the procedures we were using and many long communications about him with London (and tests to verify his competence and record his 'fist'). André was frequently copying messages in my stead, and finally quite often even handling scheduled transmissions, either with tacit, informal consent from the Home Station or possibly, in view of the security lapses SOE suffered at times, without their realizing it was not me they were dealing with. Though approving of his patent technical skills, Home Station never officially recognized him as my official replacement, since by the time he was trained and London came to a decision, they apparently felt that the W/T operators who had dropped in with our various visitors provided sufficient backup in the region. He nevertheless remained most useful in unofficially taking over almost all the tedious, time-consuming cryptography, initially limited to decoding but finally encoding too. He had no knowledge of English, but did the work faithfully and well, eventually handling a good portion of the transmissions. I still retained control of the safety identifiers inserted into each message. I had thus only to control the coding material and to do relatively few scheduled transmissions. I had managed to transform myself into Staunton's personal reserve communications link. This suited me perfectly since, in addition to my part-time reception committee work during full moons, I would now be allowed on at least limited operations. They started quite unexpectedly.

Our requirements for materiel kept overtaking availability despite the rather heavy night traffic into our DZs, though we still managed to keep German troop movements from the south from having any effect on the Normandy operations. Elements of the SS Panzer Division *Das Reich* had started moving out of Bordeaux on 8 June and the division was still struggling through the Dordogne around 20 July. To our relief and pleasure we were notified about 11 July of another daylight drop to help overcome our high usage. This time it turned out to involve only half as many planes, some thirty-five. The preparations involved almost identical arrangements: the same set up of fires (but no flashlight this time) and again the choice of a large DZ on a sort of wide, open plateau. But this time the DZ was quite near Sussac (my base of operation) near Saint-Gilles-les-Forêts, the original home base of Guingoin. We felt confident that the same means of transporting all materiel would be sufficient for the smaller drop, especially since we really had no other options. Even the reception committee was the same, and we were certain that this time it would not be submerged with kibitzers since a day drop was now no longer such a great event. Confirmation by Broadcast set the drop for 14 July, the national holiday of France.

There again was the throbbing, high-altitude approach of the B-17s and the P-51 Mustangs' buzzing salute, and in almost every respect it was very much a repetition of the previous drop. Though the crowds were much smaller we still had problems keeping firm control, since it turned out most of the extras were there to obtain parachute material for wives or girlfriends. As if pre-ordained, a similar proportion of the containers, whose static lines had been left unhooked (or badly so), came crashing down, and again we had some exploding ammunition as one container landed in the fire at the head of the line. I suppose this could be seen as a testimony – unappreciated at the time – to the accuracy of the Norden bombsight. There was, however, nothing repetitive or boring in the cloud of 'chutes floating down so peacefully. This remained a tremendously impressive sight, especially since they were suspended in the air for so long due to the altitude of the drop.

We had the same problems of drifting off site and searching for and collecting boxes back to the DZ. We did the same sorting of the

410 or so containers, allocating them to specific camps, but it went far more slowly. We wasted no time but there was no sense of novelty or great urgency as most camps still had some operating materiel on hand. Although the whole process had become somewhat routine, there were far fewer persons doing the work since so many were occupied ambushing the German road traffic, which was the preferred occupation. Many containers were opened to verify contents and mark them for specific destinations, as were the packages that dropped in separately. One of these packages (addressed to me) contained a complete spare radio set (minus crystals), a bag of rice, and best of all, a large chunk of wonderful semi-sweet chocolate.

At the end of the day much of the drop was still strewn across the field, minus parachutes and had at least been collected from wherever it had landed, even it was far from ready for transport and distribution. There was no doubt that 'tomorrow is another day' was the prevalent feeling. I went back to Sussac with my radio and goodies, and went to check on André's routine decoding, savoring some of the chocolate, a rather small piece of which I ungenerously managed to part with and share with him.

The next two days were slow, both in getting started and in accomplishments: it must have been almost noon of the first day before we made any significant progress in the sorting, shipping, and removing traces of the containers. The following day's performance was still rather desultory and relatively little was accomplished, primarily because many of our trucks were having all sorts of minor mechanical problems and, unbelievably, because of a temporary charcoal shortage, for they all had large tanks attached to them in which charcoal was burned and whose fumes powered the engines in a desultory way. There was little gasoline; what little there was we used for a few cars and to clean weapons. Approximately half the drop still had to be moved and distributed.

There was a distant sound of gunfire the next morning (17 July), and we soon learned that the Germans were attacking. The first thrust came from the southwest and was eventually stopped near La Croisille, but a little later in the day we learned that some 2,000

Germans were moving towards us from the southeast, from the Millevaches Plateau area, and were reported near Saint-Merd. By afternoon, we learned of further attacks coming from the north, southwest, and east. New attacks were reported from the west around Linards, and those from the east were being held off at Beaumont. We seemed to be under attack throughout our area. The daylight drop seemed to have been the trigger; yet we had had an even larger one before and no German reaction. In our minds, we immediately identified 14 July and its strong patriotic associations as the probable cause of this retribution by the Germans. Such a blatant act on that day demanded a strong reaction and, of course, we blamed and cursed whoever it was who had had the foolish idea of scheduling that drop, thereby upsetting our established existence and threatening our *maquis*. The continued presence of the Panzer Division *Das Reich* in our area made it perfectly natural that elements of it be used against us, who were in part responsible for many of the Germans' difficulties.

The next two weeks saw some desperate, very hard fighting, a great deal of it a position-type warfare, particularly in the defense of the DZ until it was cleared, rather than our normal, fluid guerrilla tactics. Four days after the drop, the Châteauneuf positions were under great strain, and the attack from the Saint-Merd area was pushing us back onto ourselves toward Eymoutiers. For the following two days, the Châteauneuf *maquis* held, and was still holding when some 1,500 SS troops and 500 *miliciens* finally occupied Eymoutiers a week after the drop.

There seemed to be a slight letup in the pressure on us. What really was happening was that we had finally cleared the DZ and were choosing where and when to fight. Nevertheless, the military crisis became even more generalized. New attacks that had expanded on a small scale in the Haute Vienne and Creuse now involved parts of the Dordogne and Charente and the Vienne departments, and were continuing on a large scale from the south to the north of Corrèze with two other columns converging there. Yet two and a half weeks after it had all begun, it was pretty much over and we were harrying them as constantly as ever. Their estimated three to four hundred casualties had not gained them much. The civilian population of the area, however, had been terrorized. Tulle and Brive, in particular, suffered greatly from German reprisals. In the worst case, every tenth man of a large, randomly-selected portion of the male population was shot. Since liberation now appeared to be more than a possibility, the action did nothing to subdue the population and, instead, our numbers increased, as did the support for our operations.

The German invasion of our territory had come as a complete surprise, though not really unexpected. Just before the drop we had received members of the 'Tilleul' mission, who were to operate south of us, and we had escorted them there. We had also requested some shock troops and were awaiting word of their availability. We were getting ready to follow the instructions we had just received to do whatever we could against the Wolfram mines near Saint-Léonard and Bellac, as well as to destroy the viaduct at Pierre-Buffière. All our other routine operations were still actively being undertaken, but almost all of our numerous offensive activities ceased temporarily on 17 July.

I had been planning to go to the DZ that first morning, but the sound of firing from the nearby La Croisille worried me. I decided to hide my new radio set to be on the safe side and tucked it away in the bushes behind the house. André had been absent for some time. He had decided, like I had, that participation in some action was most desirable. After waiting a while to see if Staunton would come, I decided the DZ was probably where I would most likely run into him. I packed my old set in its suitcase and, with my crystals, schedules, and codes, walked there as quickly as I could. I met with him briefly later in the day just as he was leaving for the Madrange area, and he gave me several messages to send, saying he would contact me later in Sussac. Since André was away with some group, I went back to my place in Sussac, leaving my set at the DZ, having coded and sent messages from there, one indicating the situation and another stating that we were ready to receive shock troops, which would be a great boost to morale.

Later that day and the next, from Sussac, I cancelled drops to several DZs which were now inoperable due to enemy activity. For some forgotten reason, I overlooked hiding the new set, which had become my habit after every use. The gunfire seemed no closer but more widely spread. I decided to go back to the DZ and found that they could use my help, many of those originally there having reported back to their units. The remaining containers were numerous and, in view of the situation, when we were not loading them onto trucks and carts, we started moving them and hiding them in brush and ditches. Late in the afternoon some trucks that had left earlier for Saint-Yrieux returned with their loads and the disturbing news that we were cut off from the southwest portion of our *maquis*. They were sent to other areas still believed to be accessible.

After a fairly routine night in Sussac, just as I was getting ready to return to the DZ, I heard a truck approaching. It was moving fast, not at the slower pace of our charcoal-powered ones. I caught a fleeting glimpse of *feldgrau* through the hedge as it slowed to make the turn to my house. I grabbed my set of crystals, codes, and schedules and left through the back window as the truck turned into the drive to the house. I heard shouts of 'Raus, raus' as the Germans jumped out of their truck and I ran for cover in some thick brush and a fringe of trees. I could hear them as they went through the house and their happy exclamations when they found my rice and 'schokolade'. They left quickly, taking the radio set with them as well as all loose papers, leaving behind (for some unknown reason) only a small supply of spare paper pads. Obviously, the source of my transmissions had been pinpointed, perhaps by that plane that flew over almost every day. I was a bit shaken, and at the same time rather flattered, I suppose, to have been the target. As soon as the truck headed off, I set off (perhaps over-cautiously) working my way through the woods, circumventing the village, to get back to the DZ, when I ran into some twenty of our men. They said they were going to help another group that had stopped an armored car to set up a roadblock. I suspected they were in reality just going to look at the vehicle and, being just as curious, I followed them.

Not much later, we reached the place where bazooka fire and Gammon grenades had stopped the armored car. It lay almost on its side across the road. Inside it, among the wreckage and mess, were a couple of bodies (the first I had ever encountered), and while my companions were rummaging around for souvenirs and discussing the events of the moment, I learned that there had been two survivors who were taken prisoner. They had been turned over to be guarded by some of our wild Spanish Republicans who had taken them aside some distance. I went there with the optimistic intention of trying to interrogate them with my very limited one year of freshman German. When we reached them, we found the prisoners seated, feet bound and hands tied behind their backs, and primacord explosive wrapped several times around their necks. The guards were sitting down to drink wine while a very long, slow fuse had just been lit. There was a tense moment before I, backed by enough of the other men, was able to prevail, and the Spaniards reluctantly agreed to let the prisoners live. The prisoners became cooks in one of the camps.

Shortly after the prisoner problem was settled, we heard another motor coming from the opposite direction as if to meet the armored car. Soon we caught sight of a single *feldgrau* truck coming up the hill. Someone who had picked up a Schmeisser machine pistol handed me his carbine, and I quickly joined in the ambush that was hurriedly being set up. When the truck came around a curve in the road and its occupants saw the armored car, it skidded to a stop, much further away from us than we had anticipated. As troops jumped out, we began firing, and under very heavy return fire the truck backed up out of sight. Under good covering fire, the men effectively retreated around the bend in the road and drove off under a final burst from us. The entire engagement had lasted only a brief moment.

The men now worked at setting up a strong roadblock with the armored car at its center, following a new approach to combat that seemed to have just been passed down, that of trying to hold a position or at least cause an effective delay to any enemy advance, instead of the hit and run tactics normally used. Still excited by that brief firefight, it nevertheless seemed to me that I should get back to the DZ, which seemed more central to the action, and where I was more likely to find Staunton. So I left them reluctantly and was quite satisfied with myself after returning the carbine.

When I finally got back to the DZ, I told a man who seemed to be in charge about the armored car and the other truck. He swore and sent someone to inform someone else. He seemed quite well aware of the various threats developing around the *maquis* and strongly maintained the overall importance of holding until the DZ had been cleared. He calmly told the small group remaining to keep loading what trucks and carts were available and get them out. I pitched in. There was no doubt that we were being attacked for we could hear small arms fire. Since it was possible the vehicles might not be able to move everything out, we continued carrying some containers off into the nearby woods (some six men to each container), hiding and camouflaging them in ditches and hollows and in thick brush. I'm not certain what, if any, means were being used to keep track of where they were being hidden. This was not (for the most part) the temporary expedient we thought it was to be, for a good many of them were not moved again for some three weeks, to *maquis* to the south of us.

Late in the afternoon I was still helping move containers when a runner appeared, asking excitedly for ammunition, grenades, and reinforcements to assist his group, which was heavily engaged by a German force. The Germans were seriously threatening another road some kilometers away that was important to the transport off the DZ and to the defense of the DZ itself. About a dozen men grabbed weapons to help. Rationalizing that the confrontation was in the general direction of where Staunton was thought to be, unthinking, perhaps irresponsibly eager and feeling I had had enough of moving containers, I grabbed a Bren gun straight from a container, loaded a couple of extra magazines and followed the group. I was still carrying my codes and crystals. The radio had been carefully hidden between two rocks off the road.

We had complained often that we had no gasoline or other cleaning material with which to remove cosmoline and had asked for
weapons that were free of the stuff. Our complaint had partially
paid off this time: my Bren was sufficiently free of cosmoline to be
in a serviceable condition though it was still sticky enough not to
pass any inspection. We all climbed aboard one of the trucks along
with extra ammo boxes, some grenades and even bandoliers. I have
no idea where we ended up after a tense drive over backroads I had
never seen, but the sound of fire grew louder as we finally arrived
and detoured to stop on the gentle reverse side of what appeared to
be a small hill trailing down from the higher mountains. The runner
wanted to lead us to his group at the base of the slope on the other
side. I'm not sure why but I suggested, and others agreed with me,
that it might be more advantageous to head for the top of the slope.
From near its top, flanked by two steep, sharp rock projections five
hundred yards apart, we looked down through a relatively open
forest descending a rather sharp and deep incline. It was at the base
of this steep hillside that a large contingent of Germans and a *maquis*
group had blundered into one another at the road across the base of
the hill and were actively engaged in confused movement.

We went down midway, and from our position slightly above the
fray we added our fire into the German flank, which gave the *maquis*
force the cover they needed to stop what seemed to be a German
attempt to flank the roadblock from higher up on the slope we
commanded, the other side of the road being partially protected
by the steepness of its incline and a small area of swamp and heavy
brush. The men down by the road managed to extend their position
a little up the slope and our group joined forces with them, firing
down on the Germans from the hill. That short firefight forced a
German retreat, but as usual it was methodical, and they maintained
aggressive contact as they moved back, still probing other areas of
approach in the process. It was close to sunset when they finally
broke off. All my introductions to combat had been from quite a
distance, yet the excitement with its rush of adrenaline seemed to
have easily overcome any consciousness of fear, though I know that

most of my tension must have resulted from strong fear. The action still had many of the characteristics of a training game. In fact, some of the training exercises had been scarier, even though one was not a potential target. There was the definite satisfaction in having actively participated and having accomplished something. I had a good conversation with the leader of the roadblock group, who had been with the group going to look at the armored car. He thanked us for the help, and we briefly discussed how to improve the effectiveness of the defense. Before returning to the DZ, we helped cut down more trees across and around the road and left the group our ammunition, though for some reason we did not feel at all certain that the Germans would return to this spot.

That night trucks and farm carts were loaded as quickly as they became available, and we napped between the agonizingly few round trips. I also had a very brief contact with Staunton, who sent a message to London stating that, despite all his entreaties and insistence, the *maquis* was determined to hold around Châteauneuf rather than have a fluid defense, and he expected it 'to go bust', possibly catastrophically. I was to remain in the general DZ area making certain that the material was distributed or saved, and he would recontact me. I was getting very proficient at tossing an antenna into a tree and doing my transmission crouched uncomfortably on the ground.

The next morning we were still struggling to move containers off the DZ, or hide them, perhaps less than an eighth of them still remaining on site. It seemed the weather was becoming very warm. Since dawn we had again been hearing shooting in more distant parts of our territory. Again we got word that there were now concentrated attacks from the SE, SW, and N on our territory. There was now no doubt in our minds that the large number of parachutes in daylight (the number perhaps exaggerated by reports) and perhaps the national holiday date of the drop, is what had attracted German attention: there was a definite possibility that this represented an airborne attack requiring counteraction, since it could have been a precursor to the start of a southern invasion, whose preparations they undoubtedly were well aware of. The presence of the Panzer Division *Das Reich* in the area, still fighting its way north at the time, also no doubt contributed to the Germans' activities. When it became obvious that there was no invasion, they took the opportunity, not to mention a needed expediency, to put down our known destructive and disruptive actions.

This distant firing was coming closer and reports were coming in of several critical attacks on the approaches to the DZ area, the heaviest being near the Forêt de Châteauneuf and involving areas leading to it (one of which was near the preceding day's skirmish), which turned out to be much closer to the DZ than the circuitous route we had taken the day before had led me to believe. Again, requests for reinforcements and ammunition soon came, and many of the remaining men rushed from clearing of the DZ to help in different areas. I moved with the others, joining a group of some twenty or thirty who had been occupied in a more distant part of the DZ. We headed for yesterday's area in a very small truck. We took the time to pick up some broken-down containers of ammo to take with us.

Having noted the jutting promontories overlooking the steep hill the preceding day, I suggested again that we head that way. After a climb made arduous by the containers we were bringing and the morning heat, we reached the top of that position. On arrival we found that the Germans had the advantage, and that only one of the promontories could be of any use to us. We were greeted from below by confused shouting and firing, the German numbers and firepower seeming quite superior to the *maquis*. The roadblock area had, in fact, been overrun and changed hands and was serving as protection for the Germans. We were barely holding on and fighting off what seemed to be flanking movements on both sides of the road as well as simultaneously (partway up our hillside) holding off the enemy, who were in the process of climbing to outflank the *maquis* position, working up the slope from their own rear furthest away from the roadblock. We obviously had to hold the high ground. I shouted that the other holders of Bren guns in our group should take up positions around the rocky abutment and started to head for a point that seemed to me would be most effective to thwart the flanking attack. Being the American who had parachuted in to help, I found myself almost automatically and frighteningly accorded a certain authority, all the others assuming I had more experience in such matters than I actually did. I had indeed had good training, but never been in combat, while some of the others had. I was really concerned and frightened about making the right decisions. Also, this was to be a different kind of action, one of holding rather than hitting and fading away.

As a sort of 'by-default' leader of this sub-group, I directed with as much confidence as I could muster. I decided that many of us should position ourselves in the upper portions of the slope above and past the overcome roadblock to establish some depth to the *maquis* positions and possibly to cover any retreat of those already engaged, if necessary. I disposed the men accordingly and also sent several past the promontory furthest to the rear of the roadblock in case the flanking movement expanded there (as seemed possible). I went to the promontory with them and, as other men hurried down, I urged them not to bunch up, pointing out particular spots where they might be most effective. I assigned two men to be runners and two more to distribute the ammo and grenades we had brought and to go after more using the truck we had come in. From my position near the edge of the promontory, I could see our second line forming behind rocks and trees and providing supporting fire, but tree foliage tended to obscure some of the fighting at the bottom of the slope.

It seemed to me that greater pressure could be applied to the rather exposed German rear and flank from partway up the hill than we could accomplish from our positions. I led a small group toward the rear of the enemy flank and with grenades and automatic fire-power we forced them to withdraw down toward the road, where most of the *maquis* force was still concentrated, and from which they took some cover behind the roadblock. Since our presence above was critical, I immediately moved the group back. In some relatively quiet moments after the initial attack, I realized that the enemy (all wearing German uniforms) were speaking several languages, one I had never heard before, but that it was in German that all the commands seemed to be issued. I told the runners (no doubt superfluously) to pass the word to concentrate on officers and noncoms since these must be the German speakers. It was also in one of those brief moments of relative calm when the enemy seemed to be regrouping for another attempt that I realized I had not for an instant thought of the risk I was running for the communications of the entire operation, since I had forgotten that my schedules, showing date, time, and the frequency to be used as well as my codes and crystals, were in my pockets. The radio was still at the DZ. I worried about it briefly, even feeling guilty at the fleeting vision of the enemy triumph if they found my body, but there was not a thing I could do about it now, and I was too tense and absorbed to worry about it further. We were all starting to suffer from thirst, for no one had thought to bring water. I asked one of the runners to bring some back the next time he went for ammo and also to let me know the status of the DZ clearance.

The relative calm that settled over the area after the initial furious firefights, resulting from our arrival and the probing by the Germans, did not last as long as we all would have wished. I had the opportunity to work my way down past the roadblock and conferred with the leaders there, discovering that we had perhaps some 500 men involved. I stressed that they should concentrate their forces on the defense of the road and the other side of it, and we would move some of our people down to take care of the hillside from our higher position. I also hoped to be able to make the roadblock untenable for the Germans. We all felt confident that this concentration of effort would help, and they hoped that I would be able to get them supplies, ammunition, and possibly reinforcements. I explained that I would send down whatever I could in terms of ammunition and had assigned a man to go back and resupply us, but that we presently had to make do with whatever we had. For all the heat of the action, I discovered we had very few wounded. As I worked my way back up, I reassigned men to positions lower down, as promised.

Since we had not been dislodged by late morning, as the summer temperatures rose, the Germans brought up some sort of heavy weapons contingent with more machine guns, which could better support their renewed attacks with covering fire, and it seemed some new troops. We were slowly forced back toward our secondary position under very heavy fire, but there we held (with the help of many grenades). The Bren gunfire from the promontory did its best to counter the machine guns, but we were frequently silenced for short periods by the sheer volume of fire thrown at us. Our standard weapon, the Sten gun, had neither the range nor the cyclic rate to compete except at quite close quarters.

The next period of respite was not very short. We did our best to distribute ammunition and grenades under covering fire but, unfortunately, we were unable to provide water, which was as much in demand as ammo. Then the Germans brought in the mortars. The shells exploding in the trees greatly enlarged the area affected with falling branches and shrapnel. Most of our casualties occurred then. It was for me a most terrifying time. I found myself at times crouched closely against the biggest tree trunk around, almost hugging it, hoping the larger lower branches would provide protection, and hoping my nearly vertical position would offer a smaller target to the mortar shrapnel falling on us. At the same time, I was constantly changing my position to try to counter the machine gun fire, quite often uselessly and instinctively ducking in anticipation of the explosions. As the mortar and machine gun fire moved up the slope, the German troops followed it. It seemed to me that the attack was particularly targeting our positions on the high ground and abutment from which we maintained as aggressive a fire as possible, moving position often to be able to keep firing down and in enfilade, which was nevertheless effective in finally stopping them. By mid-afternoon, the firing had become desultory and sporadic, all positions seemed stabilized with the enemy's most advanced positions at a point less than a quarter of the way up the hill and the majority of their men still down by the road in ditches, behind two of the smoldering trucks, or still protected by parts of the roadblock. We expected them to leave as they had the day before, but instead the mortar and machine gun fire started up again, heavily. It did not seem to be intended as support of any forceful attack. Shortly, the suspicion that it was to occupy us and divert our attention was confirmed when firing started on the other side of the promontory, where I had thankfully assigned two or three men. I scooted around to that side, calling for reinforcements to support the few men I had already positioned there and started firing at the enemy troops that were already well up the slope almost unopposed. We managed to stop them by sunset, but we were extremely overextended. We were waiting expectantly for them to leave, but they settled in for the night. No one seemed to have dug in (no tools being available in our case). Cover existed only behind natural extrusions. Everything quieted down other than an occasional shot fired at what may have been thought to be some patrol action.

It was then that the runner drove up in the truck with ammunition, grenades, and even a few reinforcements. Someone on the DZ managed to get food and, especially important, drink too, which was perhaps more appreciated than everything else, for none of us had had anything to drink all day. While there was some water, most of what they brought were bottles and small casks of wine and cider. I did worry a little about having thirsty men drinking wine like water, but there didn't seem to be any bad effects. The runner reported that he had been led to understand that the DZ was almost completely cleared and would be only an empty field by midday the next day, and morale was boosted by his news that by then more help may be coming, and the wine. I sent him back at once for more supplies. A few wounded were removed and the too few reinforcements distributed where it was thought they might be needed and effective in the area of the last attack.

In view of the good news, I was starting to revise our courses of action while I checked the positions and oversaw distribution of the supplies. I had a long talk with the 'roadblock' contingent and joined a conference of all leaders to discuss the possibility of breaking off contact with the enemy in view of the DZ clearance. There was complete agreement on that, but much more discussion

Clockwise from above:

1 Jean Claude's first year at Harvard, 1942.

2 Jean Claude drafted in 1943. He had almost completed basic training before being assigned to SOE.

3 Jean Claude, Christmas 1944, in Northampton, Massachusetts.

4 Winterfold House, Cranleigh, Surrey, home to the SOE Student Assessment Board and Jean Claude's induction into SOE. (Mark Yeats)

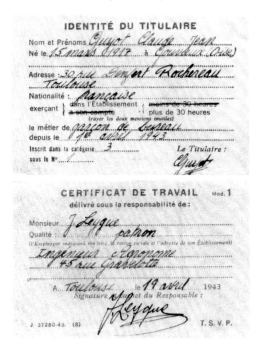

5 Jean Claude's wallet ID and certificate of employment.

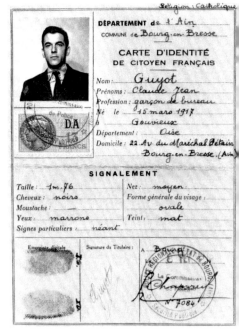

6 Jean Claude's fake ID card.

MAP 3

FORMER F SECTION CIRCUITS ACTIVE UNDER EMFFI AUGUST 1944

7 Map of France showing where the Salesman circuits operated.

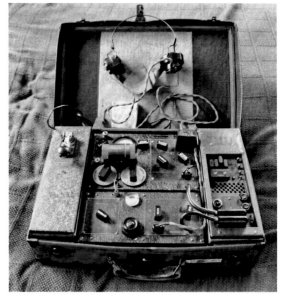

8 The type of radio set Jean Claude used: suitcase set Type 3 Mk II B2.

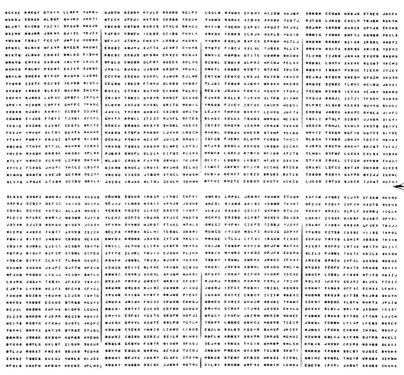

[3] **HOME STATION to OUT STATION**

9 Code sheet England to Jean Claude.

10 Equipment air drop to Salesman II, 14 July 1944.

11 A destroyed street in Oradour-sur-Glane, late July 1944. To this day, the village remains in its ruined state as a memorial to those lost.

12 Village square of Sussac, where Liewer, Maloubier, Szabó and Guiet spent their first night in a safe house after parachuting into France.

13 Group in Sussac, including unknown visitors from British HQ. *L-R:* Major Charles Staunton, -?-, Jean Claude Guiet, Philippe Liewer, -?-, -?-, -?-, André, Bob Maloubier, Jacques Dufour.

14 Jean Claude driving one of the first Jeeps flown in after the liberation of Limoges.

15 Philippe Liewer and Jean Claude Guiet on the way to the awards ceremony.

16 September 1944. After the liberation of Limoges a ceremony called *Prise d'Armes* took place in the Champs de Foire. SOE on the left and Maquis on the right.

17 Jean Claude receiving the Croix de Guerre. Philippe Liewer and Bob Maloubier are fourth and fifth from the left.

18 Jean Claude's tented accommodation after arrival in Hsian, now under OSS command. Reconnaissance missions were carried out in the area.

19 Training Chinese soldiers. OSS had to train the Chinese in the event of an invasion by Japan.

20 Jean Claude training Chinese troops. It took a long time for the Chinese to trust OSS.

21 Once the Chinese received good rations and treatment from their army, they began to trust OSS and get into shape.

22 Military convoy going from Hsian to Chengtu. To help out, Jean Claude drove a truck over treacherous roads.

23 Group in Hsian. *L-R: back row:* Major Alfred C. Rogers, -?-, -?-, -?-, Portuguese missionary, -?-, -?-, -?-; *front row:* Herbert Brucker, Alan Ke, Jean Claude Guiet.

24 Gertrude Alice Flaherty in US Coastguard uniform. She was to become Jean Claude's lifelong partner.

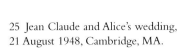

25 Jean Claude and Alice's wedding, 21 August 1948, Cambridge, MA.

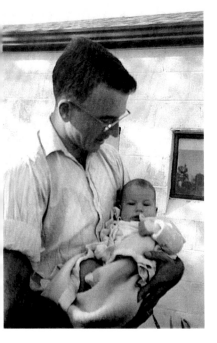

26 Jean Claude holding 3-month-old daughter Claudia Alice.

27 Jean Claude with Claudia Alice in Columbus, 1951.

28 Jean Claude with his children on the summit of Mount Tapochau, the highest point in Saipan.

29 Jean Claude and his family lived in this Quonset hut at the army base in Saipan.

30 Filipino 'fishermen' whom Jean Claude met up with.

31 Filipino 'fishermen' by their
dug-out canoe. They took Jean Claude
to meet someone somewhere!

32 The cliff from which many Japanese
families threw themselves or were thrown
when it became apparent that the US
Marines would take Saipan.

33 Bombed-out cathedral in Manila.

34 Jean Claude and Alice explore the Rocky Mountains of Colarado, 1968.

35 Jean Claude on his sailboat, Newport, Oregon, 1989.

36 Jean Claude Guiet and Bob Maloubier at the opening of the Violette Szabó Museum in Wormelow, 2000. This was the first time they had met since the liberation of Paris.

37 Jean Claude at the Limoges Resistance Museum, 2001.

on how specifically to disengage. We finally agreed to position everyone in depth so that continued firing could be provided to withdrawing troops who would in turn cover the withdrawal of those they had passed. All movement would be away from the road and as dispersed as possible. Decisions were reached as to positions, routes of withdrawal, timing, and the signal to initiate the movement, which turned out to be the setting off of several blocks of plastic and blowing whistles.

Positioned furthest from the road and with a fairly good overall view, I was given responsibility for that signal. When I was finally satisfied that we were positioned as well as possible and the men were bearing up as well as could be expected and being informed of the next day's tactics, I returned to my position, perhaps optimistically satisfied that we should (with luck) be able to hold our own. When quiet settled in (perhaps the wine had an effect, too) exhaustion hit me. I had been tense, nervous, and very frightened throughout the entire action. In fact, I was terrified by the mortar fire directed specifically at our abutment and the machine gun fire trying to silence the fields of fire of our only heavy weapons, the Bren guns. Now, perhaps due to the fatigue of the last two days' activities (no doubt extenuated by the wine), I felt at ease, relaxed, and rather happy that I had not panicked and had so far survived. I must have fallen asleep for a short time after all my checking activities because firing awoke me as the preliminary attacks resumed at dawn.

The morning started slowly as the enemy prepared to attack: we could hear trucks approaching, possibly bringing in more reinforcements. Otherwise, it seemed very much a repetition of the previous day, including the mortars, and the fact that we were again running low on ammunition. By noon, it looked like the positions in front of the roadblock position were about to fold, the higher ground on the opposite side giving way, and the rest might not hold. I could see no sense in trying to hold any longer: no need to risk more lives and surely the DZ was now cleared. I gave the 'withdraw signal' (the detonation of several blocks of plastic, which strangely enough made a distinctive sound amidst the normal uproar), and with an increase of firing, one group after another faded away from the road upon which the Germans immediately concentrated. Other than having no plans to meet in any given area, the success of the extrication surpassed all my expectations. The mortar and machine gun fire ceased suddenly, but there was no effort to follow the retreating men. It quickly became apparent why – almost miraculously, at this same time, another *maquis* group, not having any inkling of our plans, materialized in response to previous requests for help and attacked the Germans from their rear and from their flank on the other side of the road, causing a much-appreciated diversion which contributed much to our successful departure. By nightfall the Germans had disappeared. A group of us gathered and had a tired celebration, eating and drinking voraciously.

I was beginning to wonder how I had had the nerve to get as involved as I had. None of us could understand the persistence of the German attack. They could have detoured around us or reached the DZ by other routes. The only explanation we could arrive at, perhaps a little too flattering, was that this had been their assigned sector and someone in charge was not going to admit being unable to deal with a bunch of irregulars.

Staunton's approach of fluid activity now seemed to have prevailed as word was passed around the units that we were to revert to our guerrilla tactics – attack, destroy, and hinder but not hold. After food and drink, I spent a restful night sleeping in the woods. I remained with this group another day, participating in two small ambushes, but mostly I wanted to make sure that the DZ was not occupied by the Germans so I could retrieve my radio. The group had no specific sector to cover and the atmosphere was quite casual, but we were still fairly effective. The Germans were roaming our entire area pretty much at will but under constant harassment. When I finally left the group, I handed over my Bren gun to another man, managed to pick up my radio from where I had hidden it on the DZ, and took it back to Sussac.

On a scheduled contact, I received a message announcing the possible availability of a Dakota expert ('Faust') and mentioning the possible arrival of an OG (Operational Group), and requesting where and when they could be received. I had already been out of contact with Staunton for too long, but felt quite certain that with the present situation, it was very unlikely that we could receive either of them. I did not know exactly where Staunton was, but I felt quite certain that he had received the same message, knowing that he now had other means of making contact with London through the radios of some of our visitors. We finally made contact again shortly after we got word that the Germans had occupied Eymoutiers, and he confirmed he had gotten the message and been unable to provide a DZ. He asked me to recount details of my activities during the past few days and limited his comments to expressing satisfaction that I had survived and 'enjoyed' myself. I was told to stay where I was and expect him soon.

Indeed, the very next day I was picked up by a convoy of two cars, the first carrying Guingoin and two others unknown to me, and the second containing Staunton and Bob. Staunton, who had been a sort of amateur racecar driver, was of course at the wheel. During the ride there was little conversation other than comments on how serious the immediate situation seemed, how things hopefully looked like we would soon be back to our normal offense mode, but no hint as to our destination. Staunton did not know where he was going either, he was merely following Guingoin. Staunton was happy to know I had all my schedules, codes, crystals, and radio with me, and was still capable of full operation. We followed Guingoin's car for about two hours, down roads that were little more than wide paths through the woods, at one point crossing a dirt cantonal road through the dust of German trucks that were just passing the intersection. If they saw us, they did nothing and I don't think they could have followed us down the narrow lanes we took. Nevertheless, we turned off onto another lane as soon as we could. Finally we ended up in the middle of nowhere at an isolated farmhouse which was apparently one of Guingoin's communist hideouts.

We stayed there for several days, and I got an overview of the magnitude of the German attack, how Bob had been left in charge of operations around Châteauneuf and how the Germans now seemed to be letting up on the Haute Vienne, our center, perhaps thinking they had 'taken care of it' and had been concentrating more on the surrounding departments of Charente, Vienne, Creuse, and Corrèze. Meanwhile, Staunton had been trying to get up to Bellac, where he hoped to be able to receive the OG he desperately wanted, and probably the Dakota expert, whose arrival he did not want at this time. He planned to take the offensive with the OG as spearhead. There were also organizational discussions with Guingoin and his colleagues, to which I was not privy.

At times, with nothing better to do and only Broadcast and BBC news to monitor (and the occasional scheduled contact), we wandered around, never venturing too far from the farm. It was in one of these wanderings that we found ourselves close to a communal road just as two trucks stopped. For a moment we thought we were about to be attacked, but they were just stopping to give the troops a ten-minute break. They were French *milice* and 'German-allied' troops led by German noncoms. We watched the two groups light up cigarettes, stretch, urinate, and engage in normal, calm conversation. They were perfectly at ease, showing no apparent concern that they were in enemy territory. It was clear that they thought they had subdued the area. They now had the complete run of the whole area, though the *maquis* were still present, just keeping out of sight.

The German operation lasted about three weeks, during the first of which the *maquis* fought strong delaying actions and, around Châteauneuf and the DZ, a three-day virtual war of position, of which I was involved in only one sector. During the second week, the Germans had pretty much complete freedom of movement within a given area. The *maquis* all stayed out of sight and made little effort to seek or make trouble for them except for ambushes or when they moved to attack a different *maquis* sector. This may well have led the Germans to believe that we had been eradicated, even though we were resuming attacks on the rail system within a week of the start of their invasion (though less frequently and efficiently). These we conducted mostly at the perimeter of our areas of operation; on occasion, they were seriously complicated by the presence of so many troops roaming about, as were most supply drops.

By the third week, they were all but out of our area. Their main impact was the disruption of a great deal of our operational and functional infrastructure, particularly our phone system and one or two camps they had managed to locate, as well as the food distribution system. Their operation had not really accomplished much: had it occurred after the June daylight drop it could have been quite effective. As it was, they left us just in time to start their retreat to the northeast as a result of the Allies' 7 August breakout in Normandy, the sweep across France and the 15 August invasion of southern France. According to Guingoin, some 2,500 German troops, some of them SS, a majority of them Romanian and Russian, as well as some 500 French *milice*, were involved against us: they lost some 342 killed, including seven officers, versus *maquis* losses of thirty-eight. Where he obtained these figures I know not. By the first week of August, we were starting to operate at about the same level as before 14 July. The tide was obviously turning in our favor. Resupply was still a serious problem as more and more men joined as Allied victories more clearly defined political and risk options. Night drops, as many as we could handle, were still insufficient. Perhaps a little optimistically, an expert in Dakota (C-47 aircraft) landings named Fraser (code name 'Faust') was sent in. He arrived as part of the same drops as the OG we had been requesting and for which we had been trying to find a safe DZ for the past week.

Staunton, Bob, and I met them there and went to a large, isolated property (château/farm) near La Croisille, called (I think) La Vialle, which Staunton had managed to requisition. I helped Fraser's radioman make his first contacts and drove Fraser for several days in the southern Haute Vienne, Creuse, and Corrèze, helping him look for possible landing areas. I finally left him with Commandant Bernard near Saint-Junien starting to improve the airfield there. He eventually appeared in Limoges after its liberation to work on its airfield. I returned to the OGs near La Croisille to discover I had missed much activity.

The OGs were a group of some twenty Norwegian-Americans under the command of a Captain William Larson. In addition to the armaments they carried, they brought with them a surprising amount of coffee that I found not to my liking as they consumed it black and very strong. They immediately became our shock troops and also operated in conjunction with a French SAS group under a Lieutenant Le Blanc, both under the direct command of Staunton. They were occupied full-time. During the first week of August, the road and railway from Limoges to Montauban was, for all practical purposes, unusable to the Germans, and the Limoges–Poitiers and Limoges-Périgueux lines were out of service almost constantly. The Angoulême–Limoges and Limoges–Périgueux roads, and most secondary roads, were also able to carry very little traffic. London assigned a high priority to the Tours–Vierzon railway and by that first week of August some 900 meters of rail and a bridge had been destroyed on that stretch. A late attack by a contingent comprised entirely of German troops was completely repulsed with heavy losses near Villechenoux. By the middle of August (probably more in response to the invasion of southern France on 15 August than to our activities), all German files and female personnel were being evacuated from Limoges, and the Germans' primary activity now was getting away to the northeast by whatever tortuous routes they could find.

I was with the OGs on ambush duty on the main road out of Limoges when Staunton received word from various railroad sources that freight trains accompanied by a German armored train were scheduled to leave Limoges for Toulouse. We all went as quickly as possible to a suitable spot, set up camouflaged charges, and waited. By late afternoon it was obvious the train was not coming, since German trains had generally given up travelling at night now. We detonated the charges and went home somewhat disappointed.

The next morning Jacques Dufour ('Anastasie') arrived with the good news that trains convoyed by the armored train were stopped about ten kilometers away repairing a bridge before proceeding. They were trying to clear a way through the wreckage on the Salon-la-Tour line. At the same time, we learned of a second armored train that was due to come up from Brive to assist. The trains from Limoges had stopped for the night some three kilometers south of Salon-la-Tour and Staunton decided to ambush them the next morning in a cutting not far from where they had stopped. I was directed to my primary and reception committee duties that night and could not justify staying since André was attending another group, unavailable for radio duties, and there were several priority messages for scheduled transmissions. Perhaps it was just as well that I missed the operation.

The charges had been placed and by dawn, with everyone in place, it had been noticed that a concrete pylon (unnoticed in the dark) was tilted toward the tracks, the result of some previous activity. By then, of course, there was no possibility of moving the charges to a different location; the men had to hope that trains could get past the pylon. It might well have, but German efficiency precluded it. The armored train stopped and troops had deployed to cover the repair of the pylon. The charges were undetected, but some member of the SAS group had been spotted, the alarm given, and a furious firefight had developed. The attacking group had had to retreat under heavy fire after detonating the charges, receiving several serious casualties, among them Captain Larson. (His body was recovered the next day and buried with full military honors at La Vialle.) The armored train and its companions had returned to Limoges and were still there when we liberated it. The other train coming up from Brive had also been stopped, and all use of the line as well, by a blockage of several hundred tons of rock between Uzerche and Brive.

During this period, Staunton was also involved with a meeting with a M. Deschelette ('Ellipse') who was the Délégué Militaire Régional. Together they agreed to appoint Guingoin and Commandant Huard of the Armée Secrète as co-heads of the FFI in the Haute Vienne. The different *maquis* groups (AS, FTP, and others) which had existed somewhat separately while still operating under Staunton's overall direction, were now officially organized into the FFI under General Koenig and assigned four specific sectors which were covered by almost 8,000 men. While constant ambushes were taking place, hindering all road traffic in virtually every direction, there were also quite successful attempts to keep the Germans from leaving Limoges. A German attempt to get through a roadblock on the Limoges– Montauban road was for the most part successfully frustrated over a three-day period, leaving some 100 dead and many wounded before the majority retreated back to Limoges. The *milice* also tried a breakout near Grammont and they, too, were forced back.

The objective of isolating Limoges was quite definitely being accomplished; by mid-August, the outer suburbs of Boisseuil and Saint-Paul-Eyjeaux were occupied, as was Feytiat, the site of the airport, which had been rendered almost useless by deep trenches the Germans had cut across the runways. However, it rather quickly became apparent that we would not take Limoges by direct assault, and nor were the Germans ready to surrender. They had some 1,500 troops plus tanks and flamethrowers. There were even a few occasional reinforcements drifting down from the northwest. They still had a large contingent of the *milice*, which had failed to break out and must have been desperate, facing hatred and certain retribution for its collaboration. To fill a definite need, and perhaps in anticipation of more pressing immediate needs, we received an American surgeon, a Captain Agee ('Antagonist'). About that same time a Jedburgh team under captains Brown and Viguier dropped in at Saint-Gilles-les-Forêts and contacted Staunton. This team had recently participated in the destruction of the bridge at Saint-Léonard.

Staunton did not at first contemplate occupying Limoges: he was still concentrating on hindering as far as possible all German movement to the northeast, and could foresee the considerable damage to the city's population that such action might involve. He was, however, also interested (if it did not seriously interfere with the obstruction of German movement) in taking the German garrison prisoner almost one barracks at a time, disposing of the *milice*, capturing arms and gasoline, and possibly leaving a few groups to maintain order. In fact, as a result of a confusing message asking how long we could hold Limoges (whether under the misconception that we already had it or in anticipation of our doing it), I transmitted back a plan involving the FFI and requiring paratroops. The same message also requested air support, though this was primarily to be used to help stop troops trying to leave Limoges. In the meantime, Guingoin was heading Communist party activity calling for a general strike in Limoges and pressuring the head of the *gardes mobiles* and *gardes mobiles républicaines* to comply with de Gaulle's directive that all police forces should join the Resistance. This was reinforced by tracts distributed directly to those troops urging compliance, which finally occurred during the nights of 20 and 21 August. All through this confused maneuvering, *maquis* groups were penetrating and raiding parts of the city and meeting with little resistance.

Then on Sunday 20 August, Lt. Col. de La Condamine contacted M. Jean d'Albis, the Swiss Chargé d'Affaires, asking whether he would be willing to act as intermediary in contacting General Gleiniger in command of the German troops. By noon, arrangements had been made with Lt. Col. Liebich, Chief of Staff, and d'Albis verbally presented Gleiniger with terms of capitulation: unconditional surrender of the garrison with formal prisoner status. General Gleiniger refused, stating that the Vichy government was the only legitimate authority with whom he would deal, that the FFI forces were irregulars fighting a civil war, that he had no intention of involving German troops in a civil war, and would permit entry to Limoges only to legitimate Vichy troops in accordance with his orders.

Later that afternoon, a written version of capitulation terms was delivered by d'Albis to Gleiniger, spelling out that surrender would be to Anglo-Franco-American troops, that surrendering troops would be interned in a camp with special quarters for officers, that war prisoner conditions would be the same as those of Allied troops interned in Germany, that wounded personnel (while prisoners) would be left to recuperate in hospitals under Allied medical supervision, and, in a symbolic gesture, that the general would not be disarmed. Staunton informed me of this and opined (no doubt jokingly) that if any surrender negotiations were to take place, it might well be that Bob would represent Canada and I the US. I was, of course, elated by the turn of events and even more excited when that evening Gleiniger expressed thanks for a written document, agreed to discussions with the inter-Allied representatives to be held at M. d'Albis' residence and provided safe conducts for a meeting to take place the next day.

Whatever dreams I had of my participation were quickly and quite logically dashed by the need for someone of rank to represent the Allies. I watched the two Citroëns, one with English and French flags and the other with American and French flags, drive off with Major Staunton heading the group and representing England, Captain Charles Brown representing the United States, Captain Viguier the Forces Françaises Combattantes (the Free French), Captain Guery the Forces Françaises de l'Intérieur, and Bourg to do the interpreting. General Gleiniger, Lt. Col. von Liebich and Captain Noll represented Germany.

The meeting went surprisingly well, as Staunton later told me, starting at 4:00 p.m. with a slightly awkward encounter when both parties showed up at the d'Albis door simultaneously: there was some shuffling until, by quick agreement, highest rank went in first. The meeting ended about 6:15 p.m. with only a short interruption at the request of General Gleiniger to consult with his staff.

In response to d'Albis' statement that they were gathered to discuss the ten points of the conditions of surrender, Gleiniger categorically stated he was not ready to surrender and wanted to discuss the basis on which surrender should occur. Staunton, boldly bluffing and without hesitation, answered that on receipt of Gleiniger's acceptance to participate in the meeting, he had cancelled a heavy bombardment of Limoges and suspended operations against the city, which was encircled by more than 20,000 men. He added that American armored forces were advancing toward the city, and that it was necessary to avoid civilian bloodshed. He further let it be understood that he was the direct representative of the Allied Command in the Haute Vienne. Gleiniger then insisted that he and his troops be allowed to leave Limoges, which Staunton refused on the basis that it would be in direct contradiction to his orders. Gleiniger asked that HQ be contacted to rescind them, stating that so long as he felt that Staunton was acting on a personal basis he would continue to ask for confirmation of the orders. Staunton's firm reply was that those were his formal orders, and introducing into the discussion the first article of the surrender conditions pertaining to the disarmament of the German troops, he managed to direct the talks to the terms of surrender, which, with some timely diplomatic support from d'Albis, drew a somewhat grudging acceptance from Gleiniger to go over the surrender document point by point, though he made no commitment to accept it.

The ensuing discussions involved many details ranging from the twenty-three kilometers the troops would have to walk to their internment, to which troops would be involved in Gleiniger's surrender orders (all troops in uniform including Feldgendarmerie, political troops, and the Gestapo), and how Red Cross personnel would be handled. In response to General Gleiniger's question of what would happen if he refused, Staunton said he would attack. Using the pejorative 'rebel FFI', which the Germans had used, he added that he could not be certain he would be able to control the 'rebel FFI' and could not assure that prisoners would be taken alive. Captain Guery reinforced this threat by stating that the FFI were not 'sufficiently military' to comply with the immediate orders: there would probably be no prisoners. At that point, the general requested a break in the meeting to discuss these matters with his staff.

The discussion resumed about 5:15 p.m. with Gleiniger's opening statement: 'Gentlemen, I accept your proposals.' After a few brief condolences, that it was indeed a very difficult decision but one that would save many lives, the mechanics of exactly when, where, and how the surrender was to be executed were finally settled, though not without discussion of many repetitious ancillary issues, including the request that Russian medical personnel be included in the treaty (quickly settled with Staunton's reply that they could stay in uniform and be interned or get out of uniform and be free), that the troops surrender to the FFI rather than the Gardes Mobiles, with the stated preference that it be to detachments of the AS (denied by Staunton's reply that there was now only one group, the FFI). The time of surrender was finally agreed as 21:00 after several attempts to delay it from 18:00 (on the grounds that this gave insufficient time to issue the orders, countered by the argument that 18:00 had been selected to avoid a night march for the prisoners, followed by let's delay it until tomorrow since technically there isn't enough time to do everything, and finally settled by Staunton's response that technically he was unable to stop the operation).

It was finally agreed that FFI detachments would enter Limoges by the Toulouse road at 20:30 and that a German officer from each barrack would be present to escort the FFI. Anyone offering resistance of any kind would not be covered by the treaty. All weapons and materiel were to be deposited in the barracks' yards. Gleiniger's protest that the troops would have to walk to the Saint-Paul internment camp elicited Staunton's bitter repartee that he was present when English and Canadian prisoners from the Dieppe raid were walked to Rouen and were without shoes on arrival. However, he agreed that anyone over forty-five would walk only part of the way (to Crézin) and would be transported from there. To Gleiniger's explanation that his protest was not a matter of age, but rather that the majority were noncombatants and wounded from the Russian front, Staunton's retort was that he had seen the German's attack at Aixe, and they had not appeared sick. Therefore, all troops, service units, and women would walk; officers could temporarily retain their cars, would spend the first night at Saint-Paul, but the next day would be transferred to a château. Personal belongings could be taken but the men would be searched. Two last requests were granted: the surrender of Saint-Léonard would be delayed to allow time for the orders to be delivered, and the specific addition of the police troops, SD, and Feldgendarmerie would be spelled out in the treaty. The final agreement was that officers' surrender and the signing of the treaty would take place at German headquarters at 20:00.

What actually occurred bore little resemblance to what had been envisaged in the agreement. When the Allied delegation arrived at the German headquarters at the appointed time, they were met only by Captain Noll, who informed them that the SS and others had refused to comply with Gleiniger's surrender, which had been prohibited by orders received from Lyon during the negotiations. The SS had kidnapped him and were, in fact, breaking out. Staunton declared the treaty to be null and void and that the FFI would take all measures to assure the surrender of the city. Captain Noll and some three hundred troops did surrender, but the next twenty-four hours were an unbelievable confusion. The SS armored forces and others started out for Lyon, and without those fictional 20,000 men, the FFI's best efforts with 3,000 men were unable to stop them with the few bazookas and heavy weapons available. There was no air support since it was being used to support Patton's movements and the Normandy encirclement. However, we did impose serious casualties, took several hundred prisoners, destroyed a good deal of equipment, slowed their progress, and generally made their lives very difficult.

Meanwhile, in town, other German troops were shooting at each other, the FFI was attacking barracks, and the Garde Mobile (which had quit Limoges the night before) were overcoming all resistance immediately around Limoges and helping the *maquis* forces in their constant ambushing activities.

It was two or three days after the negotiations before I got to Limoges. Military activity had just ceased, but there were still many other tribulations for the inhabitants. Aside from the very time-consuming efforts of dealing with 'normal' life and the ever-present shortages and strict rationing, the excitement of the liberation devolved quickly into a post-occupation phase of retribution. This phase was rather extensive though it did not last very long. Women who had associated with the Germans were dragged into the street and had their hair shaved off in public displays to the accompaniment of bitter, vociferous insults and even, in some cases, physical mistreatment. There were also frequent beatings of persons suspected of not having been patriotic enough, of being identified as a member of the *milice*, or having in some way been associated with the Vichy regime/Germany. Some of it seemed to have been personal vendettas, although there were also the busy activities of the 'official tribunal' set up immediately after the liberation. The judgements had no appeal or recourse and sentence was executed within twenty-four hours. It seemed to be an almost round-the-clock activity and, indeed, by 1 October, when the tribunal was finally disbanded by order of the provisional French government, it had handled some 350 cases, condemned about seventy-five persons to death and many others to long prison terms or forced labor. While there were, no doubt, many instances of summary justice, most of the convicted were *milice* personnel and real collaborators. It was before one of these tribunals, I later learned, that Violette's jailer (who had led us on) ended up. I do not know the outcome of his trial, but suspect the punishment was heavy.

On my arrival in Limoges several days after the failed signing of the treaty, I found that we were to be very comfortably ensconced in the former Gestapo headquarters. I dutifully took a room on the top floor, where I could best set up my antenna, though I don't remember many transmissions and believe most operational traffic stopped shortly after we settled in. These were posh quarters: a large salon, a bar, a formal dining room, bathrooms with hot water, and two wonderful ladies who were our cooks and housekeepers. It took a little time to get used to this and to the adulation and petitions of the crowds that seemed always to gather outside our door whenever one of us would step out. Sometimes it seemed there were almost as many people inside. As could well be expected, we too had a brief but active period of celebration with several wild parties. But generally we spent time getting settled and establishing contact and communications with the various groups who were also establishing themselves in different parts of town.

And, of course, the Germans were still around. There was a still steady but diminishing stream of them flowing up from Bordeaux to Angoulême and from there toward Poitiers. Commandant Bernard's *maquis* liberated Angoulême before continuing up to La Rochelle, where some twenty-four US airmen were liberated and flown back to England from Limoges, whose airport was rapidly put into operation under Frazer's supervision, and supplies flowed in along with visitors.

I joined in the many ambushes on the roads toward Poitiers and clearing out German defensive points covering their retreat northeastward. I had the opportunity to participate often, making up for my earlier frustrations. When we were attacking around Châteauroux, we had a scary experience. We had just chased the Germans out of a château, the hub of one of their defensive positions. We watched with horror as a low-flying B-26 was hit by ground fire, the left wing exploding off in flames and the plane crashing not far away. We found no survivors when we got there. As we were assembling to leave, it was discovered that Bob was missing. There was a brief burst of firing not far away to which no one paid much attention. A search revealed no trace of him other than a sighting of him going alone toward a road at the foot of the slope beyond the château. The road was deserted. Staunton and I were a dispirited twosome as we left the group to return to Limoges. He was still very involved in the coordination of activities in Limoges: I, on the other hand, had relatively little to do and felt quite depressed at seeing the original group so decimated.

About two weeks later, I was alone in our quarters and Staunton was at some meeting when the phone rang and there was Bob asking in a perfectly natural voice (as if nothing out of the ordinary had occurred) if we could pick him up in Moulins at the Café de la République. He only admitted that he was tired, dirty, and hungry. Within a very short time I had gotten in touch with Staunton and we were both in a car speeding toward Moulins, annoyed by every delay at the numerous checkpoints that had sprung up. Staunton, who had been an amateur race driver, showed his skill in the rainy night, and I hung on with visions of some impending accident. In Moulins, we found Bob waiting in the café and immediately started on the return trip, but at a more sedate pace.

Bob was indeed a lucky man. He had gone down to the road to see if there was any traffic on it. Coming over the crest of a hill, to his delight, he saw two or three helmeted Germans pushing their bicycles with the setting sun behind them. Rather carelessly and impatient, Bob stepped out casually holding his Marlin and politely said, 'Hands up, gentlemen, please.' As they complied, he was only then aware that immediately behind these was a whole small convoy, now alerted that there was trouble. Bob was wounded in the arm by a burst of fire (the burst we had heard), but his British officer's uniform saved his life.

He was quickly captured, tied up, and placed in the back of a small pickup, where he was jammed between two fifty-gallon drums of petrol and some artillery shells. Bob could personally vouch for the demoralizing effectiveness of our ambushes. The small convoy was continually attacked and delayed, and Bob had visions of the drums exploding into flames. Other than his predicament in the truck under ambush, he was fairly well treated, ate the same food as his captors, whose primary interest was getting east, and he was not bothered by more than a very cursory interrogation. When they finally reached Moulins, after several particularly heavy ambushes, the German officer in charge realized that they had no means to care for their many wounded, who would also hinder their chances of getting through. He offered Bob his freedom if, as a British officer, he would undertake to arrange for their care, safety, and formal surrender to the FFI. Bob very happily agreed to this, setting the wounded up in the care of nuns and local FFI, and then called us.

There was a break in the ambushing activity about mid-September. Bob had returned to us at the right moment. A large *prise d'armes*, a military review, in which many units of the *maquis*, each outfitted (I never discovered how) in different, new, snappy uniforms, passed in review before the newly appointed Prefect of the Haute Vienne and medals were awarded. All three of us were decorated. I received a Croix de Guerre with Bronze Star for participation in a large, successful ambush earlier in September at Saint-Michel-en-Brenne. It was my first and only such ceremony and I found it quite impressive.

Shortly after Bob's safe return, Staunton (in compliance with instructions from London) began to close down the operation, which is when I discovered it was called 'Salesman'. I later discovered that Staunton had led another, earlier 'Salesman' operation around Le Havre. I also got special permission and ten days' leave to go see my grandmother in Conliège in the Jura. Armed with several special passes, I set out, perhaps too optimistically, carrying an advance of back pay to help her buy supplies on the black market. I did not get very far. I was continually stopped and delayed by FFI forces, jealous of their new authority and very suspicious of a French speaker claiming to be an American and armed with French passes. As I got further east, I was warned more and more forcefully that there was serious fighting ahead with the Germans working their way east and north. I was finally forbidden to go any further at a point where I could hear heavy and almost constant gunfire. I decided I might never make it and instead placed a good sum of money in a small parcel. The post office assured me that mail was still getting through, though irregularly. It was a gamble, and grandmother never received it. The return to Limoges was much swifter and trouble-free; I was remembered at some checkpoints and 'welcomed' as the bearer of updates on the situation up the road.

Three days after my return, Staunton had completed all his closing out of the operation, and the three of us left on about 22 September for Paris in a luxurious 'requisitioned' Hispano-Suisa convertible which we had located in a neighboring château. The requisition was formal and valid. It was an easy ride but we had underestimated the gasoline required. In desperation, we haltingly proceeded on plum *eau-de-vie*, until we came upon a stopped US army truck. The driver willingly acceded to the illegal request of three officers for two Jerry cans of gas in exchange for one of several Iron Crosses we had.

On arrival in Paris, Bob called his parents. I was invited to stay with them, and Staunton tried calling his wife, but without success, so we dropped our stuff at the Maloubiers' and promptly proceeded to a very expensive black market restaurant, casually parking the car in front of the door. As we should have expected, the car was gone when we came out since it was a luxury vehicle and we had taken no precautions. It was a shock but none of us felt any great loss: fortunes of war. We took the subway to our various 'families'.

The next few days were spent meeting many friends of Maloubier and Staunton, with long, luxurious dinners in various black market restaurants with huge quantities of champagne. I also loaned some photos of the massacre at Oradour-sur-Glane to Bob's brother, who was working with a local newspaper at the time. I was constantly having trouble with Military and French police since I was out of uniform but not really a civilian. At first it was relatively easy to speak French to the Military Police (MP) and show my false papers, and speak only English to the French police, until one day, the morning after a formal 'end of mission' dinner, I was confronted by both at the same time. They took me to some headquarters where my true identity was checked and verified, and it was established under whose authority I fell. After the MP had left, I was told that they were glad to have made contact with me again, gave me an ID pass, and informed me that I was to be shipped back to England, probably within forty-eight hours. I never got to see Staunton again, had an unsatisfactorily brief goodbye with Bob, and never really thanked the Maloubiers for their hospitality or even retained their address.

I don't know where I landed in England after a brief, crowded flight on a C-47 and becoming acquainted with my first K ration for lunch (a considerable comedown from the French cooking I had been enjoying), but I was returned to Franklin House, where I spent several days compiling a poor report covering the four months of my activities, worrying unnecessarily about accounting for expenditures and belatedly writing to my parents. I also got my uniform back from wherever it had been stored and added my Croix de Guerre and theater ribbon to my blouse. I went several times to the Baker Street office, where I was asked if I would consider another operation, an idea for which I showed rather restrained enthusiasm. In retrospect, I think the whole charade was a ploy. They were faced with the problem of what to do with the returnees. For some reason, it never entered my mind to request an assignment in France, which was probably just as well because many people with far better headquarters contacts would have been strong competition. I happily agreed to the suggestion that I go back to Ringway for a week or so while some resolution was sought. During that time, I got in seventeen jumps in the same relaxed atmosphere as the original course. Three jumps were memorable: a water jump, where we were to release ourselves from the harness just before hitting the water, to avoid being wrapped up in a wet 'chute, but I misjudged my height and had at least thirty feet of free fall before splashing in; a jump with the English paratroop leg pack, which you let down once the 'chute was open, and which did the oscillating while you and the 'chute came straight down; a jump out of a Hudson bomber, where you exited on a slide coming out just under the tail wheel and got the feeling of full gliding support from the slip stream (very smooth).

When I returned to London, my situation was settled. I was given a choice of jumping into Germany as a French slave worker or being assigned back to OSS and going home for a month before reassignment to the Far East. It was an easy choice, though I worried a little about being transferred back full-time to the OSS.

A short time later, I had orders and found myself boarding the *Queen Mary* and inexplicably assigned to a cabin all to myself, I suppose because the westward traffic at that time was light. Compared to the way out, it was sheer luxury. I reported to Washington and have a recollection of staying at the YMCA, the only place I could get a room anywhere. Compensating for that, I created a rather ego-gratifying sensation at the Navy building in Washington when I walked in unannounced and surprised my WAVE girlfriend there in the office full of female Navy personnel where she was working but, unfortunately, had no opportunity to go out with her.

Shortly after I was home on that one-month leave, Mother managed to convince some local tradesmen to relax rationing for a wonderful roast of beef. I did very little; caught up on family matters; knew Pierre was still safe; was shown off to all my parents' friends and colleagues; went on a date with a girl I had met on the *Excalibur* on our way back from France in 1940 (who was now a student at Smith College); went out with some old friends, one of whom had been neatly ensconced in the Coast Guard Academy, from which he resigned immediately at war's end; and basically had a little difficulty adjusting to the inactivity and limitations of 'home' life. I received notice that I was now a First Lieutenant.

Leave over, I left for Washington two days after Christmas with almost the same degree and mix of relief and anticipation as I had when I originally left a year and a half before.

CHAPTER 4

Back at Washington, I again am uncertain how long or where I stayed, though I have a vague recollection of once again finding a room in the YMCA. In any case, it was only for a very short time. I know I was disappointed because my girlfriend had been transferred to New York, and I could get no leave. I do remember getting several shots (inexplicably and embarrassingly passing out when given a yellow fever shot that was absolutely painless). At about 2100 hours on 30 December, seven or eight of us boarded a Milwaukee Line Pullman sleeper at Union Station and were on our way to Santa Catalina Island off the California coast for a survival training course.

I remember being bothered a bit by reactions to shots, passing through Pittsburgh, Akron, and Defiance in daylight and arriving in Chicago, where around 1800 we boarded a troop transport and stayed in the yards half the night. The troop transport was really a converted boxcar attached to the end of a long passenger train and it rode like a freight car. Other than having some difficulty getting aboard, however, it was adequate. At one end were toilet facilities, at the other end bunks, and near the middle, a pot-bellied stove. There were porthole-type windows which didn't open, but we could open the large sliding doors from the inside (although they remained closed for the first cold days across the plains). Food was K and C rations, supplemented on several stops. For the first day we were short of water and the lights failed, but that was remedied before we got to Omaha.

Knowing nothing of the US outside of the East Coast, the trip was a revelation. I still have a little black calendar diary in which I primarily kept track of when I had last been paid but also made a few notes on the trip. I was apparently impressed by the wonderful free canteen at North Platte (4 January), and thought Wyoming rather dull; we finally had some sun on 5 January. I commented on Indians seen in Ogden, and finally arrived in Salt Lake City late in the day. We were disconnected from our train, and shunted into the yards for the night. We managed to get to a downtown hotel, discovering that drinks were served only to members of some make-believe club, membership to which was easily, if expensively, obtained. I was impressed by the width of the streets. The next day we must have gone through Denver, delighted and struck by the Rocky Mountains as we passed through them; it was warm, we had the sliding doors open, and enjoyed the slow passage through tunnels, twisting tracks, and Glenwood Springs, where we stopped to let some other train through. I was surprised to see land of such grandeur with so few people. Early on 7 January we arrived at Los Angeles, appreciated the palm trees, but not the cold drive in an open truck to Newport Beach, where we boarded the boat to Santa Catalina, disembarking in Avalon almost two hours later.

We were quartered in comfortable quarters, and the very next day went for a hike with an instructor named Rocky. It was an introduction to how survival was possible with only a canteen of water and a trench knife. We started at sea level and were shown some abalone quite deep along the rocky shore, told they were delicious, but given no hint how to retrieve them without being battered against the rocks by the waves. Presumably, it was desperation that would provide the answer. We also were taken up gullies it was explained that following them down was the best way to reach water. With no water around, we were shown how to pick, peel, and eat cactus pears for their moisture (probably the most useful piece of information of the whole course), our attention was drawn to the acorns available and we were told they were very nourishing raw or roasted, and finally we were shown how to make snares to catch small game with delicately set branches, grasses, and stones. We were given a demonstration by Rocky who with his telescopic rifle shot a goat high on a crag across the valley, whose retrieval proved impossible without much mountain and cliff-scaling equipment. Our consolation was that we were told those goats usually had a very strong flavor. The following seven days were repetitiously taken up with the same type of information, expanding also into medical emergencies, through many lectures, movies, and occasional demonstrations, one of the more memorable ones being how to make a crutch by cutting a branch with a 'Y' in it with your knife. In the demonstration this was done with a small saw. So much for the trench knife. Sunday was blessedly a day of respite. After one overnight group bivouac, we were broken up into teams of five for the survival course test.

The course, I believe, required that we go to four or five separate points (I think) spotted at various tips of the island, sign in at a box in each location, and survive as best we could. At each checkpoint would be provided the location of the next one. We were given a contour map on which the first checkpoint was indicated and it was up to us how we got there. As a team we decided that since the presentation of the course left much to be desired, we would take the survival test seriously and leave with only the clothes on our backs (no extra food), canteen (with cup), trench knife, poncho, and halazone water purification tablets. We set off as a group for the first checkpoint. It turned out to be the most distant. We had studied the route closely, but scarcely looked at other specific aspects of the map. Someone had taken the pencil from the box at the far end of the windy peninsula when we reached that first checkpoint: clearly the staff did not check this location very often, as was also indicated by the windblown, water-stained sign-in sheets. Luckily, one of us who kept notes on his activities had a pencil stub. As we checked the coordinates provided in the box for our next destination, we noticed that the map we had been given already indicated it. Further examination revealed that all other checkpoint locations were identified. We could now do them in whatever sequence was best for us. It seemed that there would be some unavoidable retracing of routes to hit all the checkpoints, and we debated whether to split up to eliminate that extra effort. We decided to delay that decision, at least until the halfway mark, still thinking of doing the test right.

We ate cactus pears; drank water from stagnant pools flavored with halazone tablets, which in no way improved the taste; ate acorns raw, boiled, and roasted; were always aware of hunger; were constantly tired, soaked several nights and cold every night. It came as a big disappointment when we lay down on a nice sun-warmed sandy spot, only to discover that it turned cold and damp halfway through the night. Finally, tired of going up and down ridgelines and finding single signatures at the second checkpoint, we decided we needed some nutrition. So on the third day we chased, caught, and killed a calf that was part of the herd Mr Wrigley maintained on the island. Dull trench knives are not the best tool with which to accomplish this, especially when it is done on the run uphill. With two of us hanging onto the tail, one trying to trip it, and the other two doing our best to stab the poor beast repeatedly, we finally got our quarry. I had never before thought of how tough cowhide is. In spite of the messy disposal, we had one good meal of slices of veal roasted on sticks before a fire. Morale and optimism rose, until we discovered that we had to discard pieces we were planning to eat the next day when they obviously had gone bad. Back to acorns! In fact, roasted they were quite edible, the problem being to find some that were not wormy. I don't know whether it was the veal or just all the changes in diet, but the next morning none of us were feeling too great.

We decided then to set out in two separate pairs to sign in at two of the remaining boxes, the one who had drawn the shortest straw (I don't remember who it was though I know it was not I) to remain in camp to set up a tent in case of still more rain, collect wood for the fire, which was difficult since we were surrounded by tough scrub oak, and boil water. The last day, camping in a cold rain, but in greater comfort than ever before, we rested less than a mile from Troyon.

The following morning at the break of dawn we returned to quarters, shaved, had wonderfully long, hot showers, and brushed our teeth with toothbrush and paste, not the twigs with the ends splintered and splayed that we had been told were even better for us. Over breakfast we found to our dismay and pride that we were the only group to have completed the course as it was intended. Some groups, perhaps more clever and wanting to show their subversive expertise, had packed candy bars, sandwiches, instant coffee, and cooperatively forged group signatures at the sign-in boxes. One of the most enterprising groups had never gone to sign in, had raided the kitchen in Troyon every night, made sandwiches for the next day, and even slept comfortably in their own beds, hiding out nearby in the woods with reading material and even going to Avalon one day. The staff didn't seem too concerned about these enterprising types, although they did point out that they would not get credit for the course, not that it really mattered. While proud of our approach, we couldn't help but envy them their initiative.

The crossing back to Los Angeles the next day was very rough. We spent the night at the Rossalyn Hotel, had a pleasant evening with cocktails and dinner, and left the next morning for Washington, this time in real Pullman cars, with dining cars and even a club car. Apparently no one had anything planned for our return so, until a scheduled departure on 4 February, several of us went home for a short visit.

Almost immediately upon my return to Washington, we were put on a train to Miami, at 0400 on 4 February. We were quartered in a nice hotel on the beach with home comforts and even service we had not really expected. We stayed there five days, during which I had a toothache and, as part of the checkout routine, saw a dentist who wanted to delay my departure to work on a filling. When I stupidly insisted I had to go with the group, he pulled the offending molar, which of course was a hasty and poor decision on my part, and I have regretted it for many years.

We were a group of some eight to ten First Lieutenants with a Major Rogers in charge of us. He was quite different from most of the rest of us, having a very genteel, distinguished manner of speaking, a good prep-school and Ivy League education, and prone to mannerisms such as relating stories about 'motoring to North Carolina with Mother'. He was definitely not military. It was fairly clear that he was a product of the 'Oh So Social' contingent of the OSS, and we all believed his commission was due to his social contacts. But he was constantly fair, undemanding, did not pull rank and, while rather uncertain of most military procedures, he was no worse than we since, of course, very few of us had had any formal military experience other than our basic training.

As a group, we were a mixed batch: two of French descent, one of Swiss-German, one of Franco-Italian, and the rest of French-Canadian descent. While we were all together for several months, I was primarily associated with three of them: Leon Demers, Herbert Brucker, and Major Rogers. As has been an unfortunate habit of mine, I never kept in touch with any of them after my discharge (although one of the party, René Defourneaux, somehow made contact with me in 1996, and in 2002 Brucker and I rediscovered one another). In the little calendar in which I kept track of last paydays, I noted our various stops on that trip. I'm not at all certain as I look at the times that I ever adjusted my watch for time zone differences.

Some of us were still in winter blouse and pinks, not having had the opportunity to get summer uniforms, when we left at 0230 on 9 February in the usual uncomfortable bucket seats of a C-47. Five and a half hours later we refueled in Puerto Rico, three hours after that we stopped in Trinidad, finally landing at Atkinsons Field in British Guiana. It was hot and muggy, we all felt exhausted and spent the next day (when not being processed) either getting summer uniforms or in the pleasant officers' club.

We left at 0330 on the 11th, with a stop in Belem for refueling at 0845, and four hours later stopped for the night in Natal, where the heat, humidity, and insects were beyond anything we had imagined possible. The day seemed to have been spent flying over endless green jungle with occasional brown rivers twisting through, and there was an inescapable dread at the thought of a possible emergency landing in such an inhospitable environment. The humidity was still the topic of constant griping the next day while we awaited departure, at 0400 on the 13th, when we took off over the South Atlantic to Ascension Island in a larger plane, arriving about noon for a very unexciting and unappetizing meal. It was the lonely, desolate place it had appeared to be as we circled the steep, dark rock cliffs and saw that the runway was somewhat short with an accentuated slope to it, ending in a mountainside at one end and a cliff dropping off into the sea at the other. There had been no other place to put the landing strip and the slope contributed to stopping the plane in time and also provided additional momentum for the short takeoff, since suddenly there was no more land as the island dropped away. In some ways, it must have been a little like a takeoff from a carrier. We all felt sorry for the personnel assigned there and were all quite relieved to leave after two hours. We arrived at Accra, Gold Coast, at 1140. I don't remember much about it except that it was exceedingly hot and humid, the natives handled all services and, as could be expected, all the facilities became more primitive the farther we were from home. We had another opportunity to really stretch our legs, getting a brief glimpse of Accra, visiting a market just outside the airport for we didn't leave until early in the afternoon of the 14th.

Then it was back to the bucket seats. We refueled in Kano, leaving about 1930 (it was agreeably cool), landed someplace in Nigeria (Maiduguri, it turned out) sometime after 2200, leaving again for El Fasher, landing about 0300 for a cold one-hour layover before leaving for Khartoum at 0400, which we reached at 0730 on the 15th flying over what seemed complete desert. We enjoyed the cool, sunny ambience, killing time while they were refueling by dragging ourselves around a local market, primarily because there was no other place to go. I don't remember seeing any airport-related structures in our stops in Africa, but it must be admitted I was not in a very alert state by then. We then headed for Aden at 1000, landing at 1600. Other than noting that we had gained three hours, I made no other notes about Aden except that we stayed there forty-five minutes.

Our next landing was at Maisara (Masira) at 0200, an island off the coast of Saudi Arabia. We were issued two blankets for it was very cold at night the short time we were there. We enjoyed a 'great breakfast' in a large tent (part of the base, which seemed to be entirely a tent city) and slept until 0600, when it was beginning to get uncomfortably warm, before embarking on the final leg to Karachi, which we reached about 1600 on the 16th. I remember relatively little of all the details of this trip, for instance, the sleeping accommodations, where and what we ate and, in general, how we occupied our time, though much of mine was spent dozing or sleeping curled up across seats or stretched out with others on the floor of the plane.

We stayed three or four days in Karachi, in very acceptable quarters located somewhere on the outskirts of the city. After crossing an extensive dry and seemingly empty plain, the non-transitional introduction to Asia, with its crowds, many smells, and its completely strange and foreign ambience, was a real experience. I went to bed about 1700 and slept till quite late the next morning, then changed some money into rupees and ventured out on a borrowed bicycle, though only into the immediate prosperous residential neighborhood. When I returned by noon, I discovered that there seemed to be some question of what to do with us. After we all had had lunch with a Mr Heably, which was my first introduction to curry (which I found distastefully hot and strong), we got MP's permission to visit the native quarters in the late afternoon. We all piled into three horse-drawn gharrys (victoria-type carriages). Even before we reached the area, we were overwhelmingly aware of the smells, a combination of every imaginable and possible pungent source. The streets were very narrow with small, dirty shops crowding both sides selling everything imaginable. The filth was incredible in terms of both quantity and variety (dirt, garbage, feces, dead animals, trash), with crowds the density of which I had never before encountered, even in New York rush hour, moving about somehow without colliding, or squatting, eating, cooking, selling, apparently oblivious to their surroundings, all shouting almost to make themselves heard, to which was added the noisy bedlam of the traffic of trucks, bicycles, wagons of all types, cyclocabs, pushcarts, somehow all managing to make progress. As we passed, we were assailed by beggars in rags, many rising from their squatting against a wall, to walk after us. No one, including us, paid any attention to them. We were also driven through the red light district with small shops on the street level and stairways outside on which stood or squatted the 'girls', the stairs leading up to tiny cubicles, some with small balconies from which more soliciting was in process, the whole an unenticing offering with a definite unsavory ambience, a purely commercial air, and no privacy to speak of. Also, we could not help noticing the large numbers of ugly vultures sitting and flapping about everywhere, obviously the city garbage collectors. As a group we were none of us impressed by our first contact with Asia.

The next day we were restricted to quarters. In view of the uninterrupted, rush-rush trip out, it seemed to be assumed that we were probably destined to be forwarded somewhere quickly and the Karachi authorities did not want to be the cause of any delay. We, of course, knew only where we were to report. A perfect stalemate. We all caught up on correspondence, leaving the following morning about 10 for New Delhi, where we were told we would be taken care of. No one knew anything about us when we arrived at 1415, so we spent the next day visiting Shah Jehan's beautiful red sandstone palace and admiring the one panel of inlay stonework that had not been stolen or destroyed. We didn't see much of the town, but what we did see seemed spacious and relatively neat, though everywhere we went, there were the ubiquitous vultures augmented by a few scrawny cattle roaming desultorily about. Perhaps to get us out of our hosts' hair we were sent to Agra, taking advantage of the trip to visit the Taj Mahal. While the palace was beautiful, the area around it was littered and filthy.

On our return to New Delhi, we got word that most of us were going to Colombo and we left again for Agra at what was beginning to seem our usual departure time of 0315, spent the noon hour in Bangalore, finally landing in Colombo, Sri Lanka, then still called

Ceylon. Again, no one was expecting us, but by the next morning we had been driven out to a training camp near Galle on the southeast coast of the island. The camp was really for underwater demolition training, but at that time had no trainees. It overlooked a splendid, palm-fringed beach from the verandas of the comfortable thatched huts which were our quarters. We were made very welcome and had full use of all the facilities and equipment. We had no duties other than swimming in the tepid water, loafing, sunbathing, drinking, with occasional trips into Galle. We even took the train up into the interior, to Kandy in the cooler, tea-growing mountains. No one knew or really seemed to care where we were to end up. Then toward the end of the week there were signs that someone's paperwork might have caught up with us; our next move was in doubt until the last moment, when we were deposited in Colombo ahead of an 0500 departure the next day. I had a nagging toothache which the humid heat did not help. We left at 0700, arriving in Calcutta at 1800 after the now usual stop in Bangalore.

Once again our presence was a mystery. We immediately were made aware that personal pleasures had priority. The person meeting us had no vehicle and asked a companion if he could borrow his vehicle just to drop us off at our quarters; he received a firm, 'Impossible! I finally got a date and that's important.' Social life in the offices, when we finally got to them, also seemed to have priority over work. For some unknown reason, we were put up in field officers' quarters and rejoined by those from whom we had been separated when we went to Sri Lanka. We visited the city in the usual open taxi with two turbaned Sikhs sitting in the front seats, this overt show of strength also serving to assure payment, I presume. In spite of obvious Europeanization, it was still not too different from the native quarters of Karachi: masses of people, incredible traffic, filth, beggars, corpses being picked up off the sidewalks in the early morning, many examples of dire poverty and hunger, people living on the sidewalks, paddycakes of cow dung for fuel being formed like thick tortillas and put out to dry by women who obviously had no means of washing their hands before the preparation of food that followed, and wandering among all these throngs the thin, worn-out-looking cattle and, in the parks, the vultures.

We decided to celebrate our last day in Calcutta, for we had been told we were to be sent the next day to Detachment 101 (whatever that might be), by going for dinner to the Grand Oriental Hotel. It was indeed very ornate with large fans we had never encountered before slowly moving the air about, with a huge staff of waiters attending to our every want but one; one was expected to bring one's own liquor and, not knowing this, we were forced to drink non-alcoholic beverages. Since none of us had been paid since leaving the US, this fling left most of us without any funds: in fact, we all owed each other money since we had been borrowing constantly from whomever still had any. By the time we reached Dinjam (Chabua), northeast India, about midnight after a long five-hour flight in C-47 bucket seats, we had eighty-seven rupees between us.

After spending the rest of the night under mosquito netting in dank, musty old tents alive with mosquitoes, we left the very extensive airport facilities of Chabua the next afternoon in a heavy rain for a three-hour drive by truck to Nazira, where we spent two busy days filling out innumerable forms and getting all the equipment that Detachment 101 thought necessary, but still none of our back pay. Nearby was Sipsaga, which produced beautiful gold and silver filigree work, but our eighty-seven rupees precluded any purchases. Loaded down with our newly issued equipment (hammocks with mosquito netting, machetes, mountain troop rucksacks, and, inexplicably, down sleeping bags) we went to Area K, a processing/training camp.

We spent less than a month there. We were housed in thatched huts that were little more than a roof between banana trees spotted in a large clearing near a swift, shallow river. Everything except the mess hall was outside. The atmosphere was peaceful and I almost got to like the constant curry dishes the native cooks prepared. Like everyone else, I tried growing a beard and mustache, but the humid climate made it very uncomfortable and I was always rubbing it, so I shortly got rid of it. Otherwise, the experience was very much a repetition of Santa Catalina. We even named our tall Anglo-Burmese pseudo-instructor Rocky. The only new things covered were a familiarization with survival techniques and moving in the jungle (vines from which water could be obtained, edible plants/fruit, and eating a monkey that we shot – tough and stringy in spite of long cooking and terribly human-looking when we skinned it – and insects). We learned first-hand about ants and especially leeches that you could see crawling toward you almost as soon as you stopped or settled for a break. We quickly became accustomed to making a thorough search for them and removing them, lighted cigarette ends seeming to be the most efficient means.

Since we were told we would be involved in lengthy patrols, most of us tried to organize our packs so that we would have all the basic things we might need in or on them. The load that resulted was not made any easier to bear by the rough and very steep terrain we were led through, and it was hard to take initially, but by the time we were actually patrolling around the Naga hills and among the Kachin and even into the Shan areas, we were accustomed to it. During these patrols, which lasted three to five days, we had occasion to stay several times in Kachin villages. Some spoke a little English, the result of the efforts of Baptist missionaries. They seemed a kindly people, generous and hospitable, living very primitively. We may have contributed to their corruption to some extent with our unconscious swearing.

It was in a Kachin village that a visiting Burmese dentist worked on my tooth, which had been nagging and troubling me almost since my arrival. I was at first reluctant, but my teammates urged me on and pointed out they would be returning in two days at the most. The dentist and his Burmese nurses were set up under a roof at the edge of the village, where children, pigs, and chickens wandered around. Yet his examination was professional, his tools were sterilized and the pain was serious enough to almost force the decision. I sat down on a regular kitchen-type chair next to the drill, which was on the end of several movable arms with little wheels on their ends through which a small cable wound, which turned the drill itself at one end and was wound around a wheel powered by a foot pedal at the other. One little Burmese nurse handed the drills to the dentist and me glasses of water and a pan to spit in after rinsing my mouth, and the other pumped the foot pedal. The drill did not have the smooth operation of an electric drill, tending to vary in speed and to pulsate, but it was as painless as any other dental work I had had done. It cured the pain and I had the fillings until they were removed for root canal work some thirty-five years later. The whole operation must have been the week's entertainment for the entire village. The dentist's visit would normally attract regular kibitzers, but having a foreigner in the chair was an irresistible draw and I think all the villagers were there, and then some.

The Naga were shyer and not frequently seen. I think we were all impressed by how small they were and how strong and muscular. On one occasion, three of them appeared when we were on a break at the foot of a steep hill we were to ascend. I offered one a couple of cigarettes and, as we stood up to put on our packs, he offered to carry it. I hesitated, doubting if he could carry it and also thinking he might try to steal it, but he shouldered it with the waist strap around his forehead. I had trouble keeping up with him. At the top, we took another break. I pointed to his handmade machete with its shorter, heavier blade and bamboo-wrapped wooden handle. I offered him mine in exchange. At first he shook his head shyly, but reaching in a woven bag hanging from his shoulder (the only article he wore other than a sort of woven bamboo codpiece wrapped around his penis), he took out a small carving, put it next to his machete, pointed to my cigarettes and trench knife, smiling and thus showing his beetlenut-stained teeth filed to a point. The deal was struck by vigorous nods. I still have the little statue: a Naga carved into smoked wood with a bead necklace, sort of pompom earrings, and a few hairs stuck to the chin. His handmade machete was better balanced and proved to be more serviceable than my army-issued one. Unfortunately, my son would later lose it on a camping trip.

Toward the end of March, we got word that Burma was not to be our destination after all and that we would shortly be moving out, though to no identified destination. We arrived in Chabua again and instead of the musty tents, we were put up in field officers' quarters. It was a little uncomfortable facing majors and colonels, who looked askance at us rather scrubby 1st Lieutenants. Our first action was to rush to Finance, get paid, and settle the complicated intra-group payback of our mutual debts. It was almost perfectly normal to have someone who owed you nothing come and give you money as payment for a debt he owed someone else who was the one who owed you. While we may not have ever gotten it straight, everyone was satisfied and, in the end, I had the glorious sum of $297 with no place to spend it. Almost immediately after being paid, we were told we were bound for China. There was also an enticing rumor that we might be going there via the Ledo Road, a wonderfully different adventure that many of us looked forward to. We were perhaps getting a little too accustomed to our world travel.

That little 'jaunt' never materialized and two days after our arrival in Chabua, we attended a briefing by an Air Force Lieutenant on how to use our newly issued Air Force 'chutes, which we were sitting uncomfortably on, and how to land. I felt sorry for him as he apologized for having to brief those of us who had already jumped. As we were walking the short distance to the plane that was to take us over the Hump (the eastern end of the Himalayas), grousing about the briefer's obvious lack of actual experience, an emergency siren sounded and we watched in appalled fascination as a plane with one engine on fire came in for a landing and exploded into a ball of flames just as its wheels touched down.

The hour's delay in our takeoff caused by that shocking event did nothing to make me feel like flying just then, but we piled into the C-47, where we sweated even more while we waited for takeoff than we had before boarding. As the plane climbed, we enjoyed a short, pleasant period of cooling off. The rest of the three-hour trip we froze until we started our descent. I assume the crash landing and the overwhelming heat/humidity occupied our minds to such an extent that there was no thought of bringing something warm on board, even though we must have known we would be flying at very cold altitudes. Anything we might have warmed ourselves with remained inaccessible in our luggage, strapped down under netting on the plane floor. The only thing we could do was to stare out the windows on the opposite side at the wing, which flexed visibly in conjunction with the audible groans and rattles of the plane as it was thrown about, and to cover ourselves up in inadequate sheets of canvas, avoid proximity with the freezing uninsulated skin of the plane by leaning forward as far as the straps of our bucket seats allowed, bracing ourselves shivering against the violent pitching of the plane, tensely breathing through oxygen masks whenever the pitch of the engines varied. It was even less reassuring to turn and peer down through the windows at our backs at the ominously rugged peaks that showed occasionally through the breaks in the clouds. I had never experienced, nor ever imagined possible, a plane ride so full of twists, surges, bounces, sudden drops, discomfort, and noise. The very flexible strength of the plane, which made it seem to be twisting itself apart, the bumpiness of the ride, the cold, and the complete inhospitableness of the terrain below all combined to make me very uncomfortable, and I almost welcomed the change in pressure and the ear pains I suffered in the steep descent into warmth and Kunming.

The Kunming airport was a busy, dusty place. We were immediately taken to a mess and served ham and eggs and coffee. When we returned to ATC (Air Transport Command), we had trouble locating our luggage, but finally about 1900 we were dropped off at our quarters and had a wonderful hot shower.

We spent the next ten days in Kunming, normally a backward provincial town, but then flooded with refugees fleeing the Second Sino–Japanese War and booming as the terminal for traffic from the south. Compared to Calcutta it was clean, though it definitely had the prevalent mixture of odors I now associated with Far Eastern cities. The streets were just as crowded with a mass of poor-looking people and skinny coolies pushing or carrying everything imaginable, and in the midst of coolies with honey buckets or other large packages balanced on either end of a pole over their shoulders, threading their way through the crowds, the pompous, prosperous Chinese drove new Packards, Buicks, and Cadillacs. The black market here thrived; it was beyond anything I had experienced in France and, with money, one could find many things that no longer were available in the US: French wines, cognac, whiskeys, Leica cameras, watches, and every brand of American cigarette. The official exchange was 600 yuan to the dollar, and we quickly learned to change our dollars at far more advantageous rates on the black market.

Other than walking around taking in all the new sights and the ambience, there was nothing much to do in Kunming. It was during such a walk near the river that three of us, quietly speaking French, were stopped by a Chinese man who asked us in perfect French if we were French. He invited us to the Mission Française and in the ensuing conversation we learned that he had lived in Paris for many years. The Mission Française was a large house set in a green garden with flowers and trees. Shortly after we arrived, Dumas (real name Casnat) who had trained with some of the others in England, showed up. As could be expected, we had a great get together, comparing our experiences, and ended up in the Red Cross restaurant, the only facility approved by the military authorities. It was rather expensive and quite mediocre. Our entire group was invited to dinner the following day at the Mission Française. It was a different, very enjoyable evening in spite of some protests among us on Major Rogers' order that we wear blouse and pinks; we all felt that suntans and a tie were sufficiently formal.

Shortly after our arrival, we were all interviewed by a Colonel Willis who, like everyone else with whom we had come into official contact from the start of the trip, was not too sure what we were there for. Other than letting us know that supplies in the field were almost nonexistent, he could tell us little of what to expect. Since we spoke French, some of us asked about going into Indochina. The categorical response was that it was out of the question, American policy in the area being to support the Atlantic Charter in hopes such a precedent would encourage England to act in a similar fashion with Burma, the Malay States, and presumably India. As a matter of fact, several of our group did end up on the border. We killed time in orientation lectures, which I might have enjoyed more without the bad cold I had contracted somewhere. As it was, we learned that China was divided into regions, each under a Chinese Regional Commander. When operational, we would report to that Regional Commander, who in effect would 'issue' us men and would have to approve any operation on fixed or permanent targets. Accustomed as we were to the relative operational freedom we had enjoyed in France, we were appalled by that restrictive chain of command, the more so as it was further explained that the Regional Commander was held responsible for us, and it was certain that he would therefore limit the risk to his reputation of any failure by limiting most actions. We also listened to lectures on Chinese customs and our allies, the Nationalist Kuomintang Party under Chiang Kai-shek. There was no mention of any other party or of any hint that Chiang's government was anything but perfect.

There were several days of rumored and cancelled notices of departure suddenly followed by an eight-hour notice to be ready. The new mission seems to have been for us to save, or help save, the second of three important 14th Air Force fields, one already having reportedly fallen. We rushed around trying to draw equipment for service with something call Group 10, North China Emergency, which none of us had ever heard of. Despite the eight-hour notice, it was three days before we left early on 10 April, arriving at noon in Chengtu. We never had a chance to see the city, which was several miles from the airport, but in our thirty-minute layover I saw my first huge bomber take off, either a B-36 or B-29. Three hours later we arrived at our destination, Hsian, whose airport nearby we had been told was under immediate threat and might even be occupied. As we slowly approached for a landing we could see the large town surrounded by a square wall with four gates and a very large tower, rather like a pagoda, in its center.

We came out of the plane fast at port arms, quickly spreading out for possible combat, much to the surprise and entertainment of the nonchalant ground crews sitting calmly in the shade. As we immediately discovered, we were the only ones concerned about a possible Japanese attack. Then we stood around waiting for what was to happen next, chatting with the ground crews, and could see that the airfield was small, suitable for fighters, but was being enlarged and lengthened for B-24s and B-25s by an ant-like colony of coolies breaking rocks into small stones, which were being carried by the basketful to be ground by hand and packed down by an old steam-powered steamroller. It was somewhat gratifying to discover that our arrival had started the rumor that we were the advanced guard of an airborne division.

After two days in a tent for transient personnel, we were moved to a compound near the town. It was spacious, built of stone, and what looked like adobe mud, and had some windows; it was also home to many insects, in particular scorpions, and every morning, as we got up from our cots, we would shake them out of our boots and kill them. It was only natural, in view of the poor information that had brought us here, that we were assigned to reconnaissance missions. On one mission eastward we found ourselves in the middle an inconclusive, brief, and confusing firefight between Japanese and Chinese patrols, with both parties shooting at us. But most of our time was spent visiting Hsian, shopping for jewelry and pottery, and admiring the cleanliness of the town. Several times every day, after sweeping in front of their shops, the merchants would sprinkle water to keep the dust down (something we had never seen in India). There was still the pungent Far East odor, but less strong than in India, and there did not seem to be any open sewers, the 'honey-bucket' coolies routinely carrying excrement off to the gardens. The imperial graves with their large clay figurine retinue had not yet been discovered or, if so, I never heard them mentioned, but I was very much impressed by the massive Ming Dynasty walls and their gates that still surrounded the city and the enormous seven-story pagoda that must have been about two hundred feet high. We were told it had been built in the mid AD 600s during the Tang Dynasty to house volumes of Buddhist scriptures. For a never-explained reason, it was called the Big Wild Goose Pagoda. Hsian had been the eastern end of the Silk Road.

Some of our team built a still with foul-smelling mash in large pots. I don't remember anyone actually drinking any of the end product. Perhaps in an effort to counter such debauched activities, we were assigned time-killing duties; for instance, I spent more than a week sitting on a porch to count the number of carts of gravel that went past me to the airport construction site and to report any that did not seem to hold a full load. No cart bore any identification and other than noting the color of the scrawny horse or the sequence they appeared in, there was no way to identify any delinquents, of which there were a fair number. Like most of my companions, I noted the number only and spent my time writing letters and jotting down my impressions of China, which I also communicated in letters to Bob Maloubier, who was then in Viet Nam and Laos.

When the pony cart phase was over, we were all invited to a banquet celebrating (I assume) close American–Chinese cooperation. I remember very little of the many delicacies served, but I shall never forget the *gambaying* ('bottoms up') toasts with tumblers of rum shared with a Chinese General, despite the fact that I passed out in the truck on the way home. I also discovered the next morning, adding to the rather confused misery of my hangover, that I had lost my wallet (probably in the truck we rode home in). In desperation, I managed to get to the motor pool the next day and found it untouched where it had dropped in one of the many trucks I climbed into. I have never drunk rum since. It was also during that period that I had a brief three-day bout of high fever and chills, for which the medic gave me the standard treatment of aspirin when I managed to drag myself to see him. He opined that it didn't seem like malaria to him. He did, however, also give me some atabrin pills, which did nothing much other than turn me a pale yellow.

In an attempt perhaps to keep us occupied, we were sent on what then seemed an absolutely pointless mission: reconnoiter escape routes from Hsian. Major Rogers, Herb Brucker, Leon Demers, and I, along with a tall, competent Chinese interpreter formerly in the Chinese navy named Alan Ke, were assigned the task. It was a very enjoyable trip. We left in a weapons carrier with two fifty-gallon drums of gasoline, our packs and weapons, some 10 in 1 rations, cigarettes, and two Chinese maps. We drove over cart paths, at first through arid countryside where some wheat and barley were grown, and through small villages where women ran out to grab their children to safety. After he had calmed them down and obtained information as to where we were and directions, Alan told us they had never seen a truck or a white man before. It was seemingly country devoid of population; yet when we stopped to relieve ourselves, as often as not we were observed by rather large groups that appeared out of nowhere before we had finished and pulled our pants back up. In villages and inns we were always surrounded by quiet but very curious crowds; to say there was little privacy is a definite understatement.

Game was plentiful, and pheasants on a nearby ridge would merely move over several steps and give us another chance if we missed them. We never ate our army rations but lived off the land, stopping in small village restaurants, the entrance to which was always through the kitchen or rudimentary cooking area – not always a very reassuring first impression. We would first be dusted off with a sort of cat-o'-nine-tails and then given warm, wet towels to wipe face and hands. At Alan's direction, they would prepare the pheasants and many other dishes, and we would enjoy a leisurely, delicious meal. We noticed that Alan always refused the contents of the first pot of tea. In fact, he sometimes threw the contents of a cup on the floor. We would not have known the difference, but Alan insisted that the first offering would always be inferior and that it was almost expected that it be refused.

From the dry plains north and west of Hsian we headed west and south into mountainous country that reminded me a little of what I had seen as we went through the Rockies on our way to Santa Catalina. We stopped one night on the outskirts of Hu Shien at a Catholic Mission. It was run by a Chinese priest and an old Portuguese padre who had started up the mission some thirty-eight years before. The padre had a large white beard (impressive in China) and seemed to enjoy his peaceful life very much, his only weakness apparently being cigars, which he rolled himself with Chinese tobacco. Overwhelmingly strong, they had none of the aroma of the cigars we were accustomed to, and none of us cigarette smokers accepted any, except maybe Major Rogers, a cigar connoisseur who all but choked while the padre quietly enjoyed his.

On our arrival we had been brushed off, shown to rooms, and furnished with water, towels, and new-to-me ear cleaners – a short toothpick length of bamboo bent at one end in the form of a scoop and at the other fuzzed up into a small ball. Prior to an excellent meal, we were left alone with the padre, the Chinese politely leaving us and seeing to the dinner preparations, accompanied by Alan as always conscientiously seeking information about the region's roads. In spite of some excellent grape red wine, without doubt normally used for church services, we all had difficulty in making ourselves understood. He spoke Portuguese, Chinese, perhaps a little Spanish, and some Latin; among us, Herby (who had had several months with the pre-war army in Puerto Rico) knew a little raunchy Spanish, and I could contribute some Latin. We used many French words with an 'a' or 'o' tacked on the end, and as the wine went around we all grew more fluent.

During an excellent dinner with more wine and conversation made more understandable by the presence of Alan and a common Chinese language, we learned that the padre had never gone back to Portugal and had not heard any Portuguese spoken since he had come to China as a young missionary. He willingly answered all our questions except where the wine came from. His only response was *de montibus*. Before retiring, we asked to be awakened early, telling our hosts that we would give them an army breakfast. Before preparing it, we made a duty of attending Mass in a simple church with a rather large congregation of mostly women. While Demers was 'preparing' breakfast (straight out of 10 in 1 ration cases), Herby and I completed our scheduled radio contact, and, after some difficulty, found a Portuguese-speaking station, apparently from one of the Portuguese colonies. The padre was a bit fearful and baffled when we brought him, with the usual accompaniment of the entire congregation, to the radio. He had never heard or seen one, but as soon as he heard the Portuguese program, his eyes gleamed and his face lit up like a child who had just received some long dreamed of present. He sat entranced for about an hour, never really comprehending how this transmission of sound was happening, while Herby and I took turns cranking the hand generator. Other members of the padre's staff also listened to the mysterious olive-green box.

The breakfast was a big success and the entire mission ate with curiosity and pleasure. They were quite baffled by the fact that eggs (pork and eggs, which they loved) came in a can, as did the butter and jam. They were too polite not to taste the coffee and the cereal with powdered milk, though it was rather obvious that they did not care for it and wondered what kind of people we were to eat such a milky mush. As we were about to leave, the padre asked us to wait a moment and appeared with a jug of wine, asking us with a wonderful twinkle in his eyes if we would accept this – or would we prefer *leche* – to the amusement of everyone in the large crowd. With this send-off and a little information on local roads, we resumed our reconnaissance duties.

The information we had been given in Hu Shien confirmed a suspicion that had been slowly dawning on us. We had been feeling that the peasants and coolies we asked about roads were all stupid yokels. Alan struggled valiantly to try to determine where a given road (really a cart trail) went or came from, but either nobody knew or we would be told it ended up an unpassable footpath into the mountains. As with many others, as we followed the road the padre had told us about (in spite of the blank faces and warnings of those from whom we sought some further confirmation), we realized that they either saw us as a threat to their roads or that the official reaction to any mishap that befell us or our truck would be to blame and possibly punish them. It is true that most of the roads were, at best, far worse than any small, unmaintained backcountry dirt track of ours, and the Chinese trucks, old, never maintained, treadless tires, patched up just enough to permit their use and screeching from lack of grease (but thereby keeping away the evil spirits), would indeed have had difficulty using them. Our information sources had no experience with a vehicle as serviceable as our weapons carrier. Most of the many roads we checked out did indeed join others and did not deteriorate any further with our passing. Various pack animals, an occasional wheelbarrow, and mostly porters were the only traffic we encountered in the countryside.

In spite of 'complete serviceability' we did have difficulties with our truck over the dusty, bumpy roads. Several times when going slowly, the engine sputtered badly and lost power. None of us knew much about engines, but we finally managed to take the fuel feed lines apart and discovered that a small plunger in the carburetor was broken as was one of the gaskets. We were about six miles from Pao Chi, which looked on the map like a town large enough to have a mechanic, and we set out optimistically, trying to ignore the fact that we would have to cross the Wei River and, as usual, there would probably be no bridge. The carburetor gave out completely before we got there. We managed to continue with me sitting on one fender getting gas from the line into a can and pouring it directly into the engine. Herby sat on the other fender with a fire extinguisher at the ready. This worked fairly well, bumpy as the road was, and we managed to maintain the engine revolutions required to keep the engine running.

When we reached the Wei and the spot where the ford appeared to be, we plunged into the river in low, low gear revved up very high. We were three-quarters of the way across, bouncing over rocks, when we were forced to a stop in a deeper hole by a rock, and the engine died. With the help of some coolies Alan 'recruited', we all got out and pulled and pushed the vehicle to the other bank. Half an hour later we managed to get the motor running again and, with Herby and me again on fender duty, Demers driving and leaning on the horn, and Alan with Major Rogers shouting at pedestrians to get out of our way, we made a noisy, 'triumphant' entry into Pao Chi. By great good fortune we had the help of an alert policeman, who led us to a garage and supplemented Alan's verbal attempts to clear the road by running ahead of us and literally shoving people out of the way, for the heavy pedestrian traffic seemed completely oblivious to the vehicle bearing down on them.

We left the truck with the mechanics' promise that they would have the plunger mended and new gaskets by morning. We walked to the nearest inn, dropped our belongings on the only furniture in the room – a wooden slab that served as a bed – and, after taking out some clean clothes, we all went to a nearby communal bathhouse (of course, accompanied by the now almost-to-be-expected large crowd of the curious). I think that I knew at those times how it must feel to be a very popular celebrity, to live in a fish bowl. I know that for a while we all had visions of taking our baths virtually in public, but instead we each ended up in a separate steamy room with a large, deep oval wooden tub into which body-temperature water was being poured by the bucketful as I was undressed and directed to climb in. I noticed that my dirty clothes were being taken away just as more buckets of steaming water were added until the tub was filled neck-high. I was left to soak blissfully for several minutes when the washer, a woman almost as naked as I, appeared. She pulled a plug from the side of the tub and let some water out, then did my face, back, chest, and legs before motioning me to stand up so she could do the rest of me. Then motioning me to sit, she gave me a vigorous shampoo before rinsing me off with several buckets of water after she had pulled the plug to drain away the soapy water. I was then given a towel and by the time I was dressed, my dirty clothes were returned to me, clean but still somewhat damp.

We stayed in Pao Chi the next day, enjoying outstanding two-hour Chinese meals (for about 82 cents per person) and left about midmorning the following day after (we all agreed) a great and very satisfactory stay, the truck having indeed been repaired as promised. Several days later we were back in Hsian, catching up on what little news there was and preparing our report.

But before actually turning it in (it was presumably turned in by Major Rogers), Herby, Leon, and I were assigned to train a group of Chinese troops. We were settled in an isolated compound several miles from Hsian, with a small Chinese staff taking care of household duties, and started off immediately training our group of some twenty-five men. The training was initially limited to physical exercises. It was more a matter of acclimatization for both parties since they were fairly fit, and soon their lethargy was replaced by a surprising degree of enthusiasm: we felt that perhaps the regular rations had something to do with it. It was a strange setup since none of us spoke any Chinese that mattered and none of them spoke any English at all. Thus, our only means of communication was the faithful, effective interpreter Alan. It could be quite time consuming to give an order in English, have it translated into Chinese, and repeated by the ranking Chinese noncom, especially as further explanations of what was desired were always required (at least initially). Stopping the execution of a given order was equally difficult. We were concerned enough to start an informal course in military and, to a limited extent, conversational Chinese in the evening with Alan, and during breaks we would try teaching the troops a little English. They were far more competent learners than we were (I never managed to master the tonals) and we soon found ourselves concentrating on the easier option of teaching them English.

The training was to consist of basic infantry platoon tactics, with heavy emphasis on marksmanship and weapons maintenance, some very basic handling of various explosives and demolition, some camouflage, ambushing techniques, and cross-country movement including night activities. They seemed to be learning well, but while outwardly enthusiastic, there always seemed to be a clear lack of real motivation. Working as a team did not seem to come naturally, and we tended to blame failures on our lack of a common means of communication. We then came to realize that this conduct was the result of the Chinese army treatment they had undergone: the officers were corrupt and short-changed the men on rations, paid no attention to their well-being, considered them a class way beneath them, and were generally incompetent. The men seldom received pay for a regimen of constant mistreatment. At first we had not paid too much attention to the communication problem, other than requesting an additional interpreter, and let it fade into the background, overshadowed by the training activity, which progressed to our satisfaction. But when we were finally told of the projected operation that was to be ours, we were overwhelmed with the significance of the problem, for it seemed that not only were we training these troops, we were to lead them in a behind-the-lines operation in the Nanking area. With command and control functions limited to one person by the lack of a common language, we were very aware of how unlikely it was that this operation would succeed. We started to do what we could, scheduling many intensive English lessons in earnest. We also concentrated even more on fair but disciplined treatment, to which the men seemed to respond well.

It was at this point in the training that my association with the group ended abruptly. It happened right after our return from a hike over a mountain trail of crude steps carved into the stone bordering a deep ravine. We had called a halt at a wider spot and were joined by three porters burdened with enormous packs from beneath which hung a pole just clearing the ground. We all watched as they stopped and bent their knees slightly to shift the weight of the pack, balancing it on the pole, and got out of the harness. They were so small in comparison to the packs that we assumed the packs to be light. Through Alan we asked our troops if they felt they could carry such a load, adding jokingly that eventually, when fully combat equipped, they would be similarly burdened. With a friendly and open familiarity, very surprising since it was the first time it had occurred, they replied that they were sure they could if we could. It was the first indication of informality in the acceptance of our discipline. The porters had heard this exchange and one of the stronger looking ones offered to let us try his pack. Somewhat trapped and not wanting to lose face, we took turns, with varying degrees of confidence, to slip into the filthy rope harness. We all managed to heft the pack and take a few staggering steps before gratefully resting the load on its pole, which was better than the trainees managed. We watched with proper respect as the thin porters got into their harnesses and with a slight grunt started up the steps at a steady stride. We were still commenting on their stamina when, as we finished the hike, I was told that I was to report at once to Hsian.

There I was informed, first thing the following morning, that I was up for a court martial. The two counts of the offense were writing in a foreign language without permission from the censors and, more seriously, criticism of an ally. I was quite guilty of both, having written in French to Bob and my grandmother (who knew no English), and indeed having several times exchanged very strong criticism of the Chinese army with Bob, who had also had contacts with them. I had seen nothing in the little I had observed of the Chinese army that did not dismay me: recruits led to training in chains; underfed, ill-equipped troops, many with no weapons, following nattier officers who were making money from the sale of the company rations and renting out the troops for labor; beatings and abject subservience with never a spark of enthusiasm.

I was terribly shocked and fearful at the news, imagining myself already in the stockade. I was somewhat reassured when informed that this was probably more harassment of the OSS by General Wiedemier in command of the China Theater, who disapproved of OSS activities in his theater of operations. I was told it would be best if I were 'not available' while the matter was further discussed and negotiated. I was to go at once to the Hsian compound to get my things for a trip: I would be going in a convoy to Chengtu, which was loading at the motor pool. It was only when I got to the motor pool that I discovered I was to drive a truck, something I had never done. And I had had visions of driving the Ledo Road! I went among the parked vehicles, finally selecting one with a brass plate still affixed indicating how to shift into the various gears. As I was slowly and nervously easing my way out of the motor pool, the sergeant in charge informed me that I was to pick up a trailer and go to a loading dock. My driving performance at this point must have provided confirmation of the opinion as to the competence of the officers among many of the enlisted onlookers, as well as a basis for bets on whether or not my truck would make it.

Having flown from Chengtu to Hsian and never bothered to locate it on a map, I had no idea that I had some 1,100 miles of bad and dusty Chinese roads ahead of me. As instructed, I had a loaded carbine, a sleeping bag, and an extra canteen of water as I set out, nervously trying to maintain my position as the fifth truck behind the lead jeep (which impressively mounted a machine gun). There was apparently some fear of possible attack by bandits or Chinese army deserters. The first day's driving was on fairly flat, open ground on roads that had some sort of surfacing, and I began to feel quite competent at driving in convoy, watching the vehicle ahead of me and following its tracks as it dodged the deeper potholes. That night we slept under our trucks after a communal meal around a campfire. It was going to be a nice outing after all.

The next day, everything changed; we were in the mountains. I got a lot of practice shifting, and often held up the convoy as I jack-knifed my trailer negotiating never-ending hairpin bends, backing up to get around them. The slopes into which the road had been cut were steep and littered with the wrecks of trucks and buses that had tumbled over the edge. Similar wrecks strewed the roadside on the plateau, where speed was increased and there the problem was dust. For what seemed endless periods of time, I drove almost blindly through clouds of dust, which limited visibility somewhat like a thick fog, and I wondered how the other trucks that followed me managed with the greater thickness to contend with since it did not seem to dissipate and just hung in the air, covering the windshield and infiltrating everything. While the road was dangerous in some places, even narrower than its normal width of slightly more than a lane and a half, the real danger everywhere was the Chinese traffic. We felt constantly threatened by it throughout the whole trip, which was otherwise quite uneventful, other than the senseless shooting one afternoon of a leopard that appeared by the roadside and was chased and machine gunned by the men in the jeep.

The Chinese vehicles and their drivers were indeed a menace. I don't ever remember seeing a bus that was not overloaded to the point of being top-heavy with the freight piled up insecurely on the roof, but they were not as battered as the trucks. The 'normal'

Chinese truck that we encountered was a rather unique contraption. Originally it had most likely been a Ford or Dodge of 1938–40 vintage, but now was unrecognizable as such. The fenders, if any were left, were battered and torn. One of the headlights was sure to be missing or else dangling by its wires and banging on a dented and unprotected radiator. Just as often, both were missing and one could be equally sure that there was no tail or brake light, and seldom a radiator cap: if the driver was really on the ball, there might be a bunch of rags in place of the latter. The cab was dented, at times even missing completely, and both the back and sides swayed and creaked dangerously as the truck moved along, for they were held together with anything from baling wire to chains. The tires were worn and many vehicles had no spares. The motor often chugged on several missing cylinders, the axles cried out for lack of grease and the brakes squealed and sometimes actually slowed the vehicle down. We felt lucky to encounter them when they were struggling uphill, where they were under some control, a painfully shuddering, smoking, coughing, squealing, grunting, steaming contraption that somehow managed to run. We could then move over slowly as far as we could to the edge of the road, or, more often, even stop at a wider point in the road until they came up and passed.

It was when they were careening down a hill towards us or, worse, coming from behind, that we all felt quite helpless. When they were coming from behind, the last truck (which had radio contact with the lead jeep) would sound the alarm and we would all follow the lead jeep as far off the road as we could get, even when it meant crossing over to the wrong side of the road. There was some security in being on the side of the road nearest the upward slope since if hit you would not be pushed over the edge to crash at the bottom of the mountainside or onto the road that ran below after a hairpin turn, examples of which we saw constantly. When we passed these, we could only pull over and up slope as far as we could and hope that the angle of the truck that seemed to be ready to topple over did not project far enough into the road to get hit, and that cursed trailer was pulled far enough off the road not to cause a collision.

In some places there were the vestiges of a slight longitudinal mound left over from some long-past road grading which might almost function as a guardrail, but there was no way of telling if the road edge, often badly eroded, would hold up a truck, so we avoided it. Fortunately, our encounters with Chinese traffic mostly involved it coming up toward us, but the few exceptions were harrowing. In one instance I, and others, left the trucks where we had pulled over and climbed up the hill for better protection. How the three trucks hurtling down the hill made it past us is still beyond comprehension, though I did wonder if a fresh battered wreck seen down an embankment further along the road was one of those three.

When we finally reached Chengtu, where I for once managed to back the trailer to the loading dock with a certain degree of success, I reported in as soon as I had had time to clean up. It was a brief, to-the-point meeting. I was informed that the court martial charges had been reduced to the 104th Article of War, meaning that the penalty entailed only a fine of some eighty-eight dollars. I was told that I was being sent out of the theater of operations. I was given all my back pay, handed a box with an unexpected Silver Star medal with no citation (though I later received an official one citing the holding off the attacks on the DZ in July 1944), and handed an envelope with orders, medical records, and a receipt for the fine. I asked if I could go back to Hsian to get the rest of my things, but was denied. Within an hour I was at ATC waiting for a plane to take me directly out of the theater, wondering if the duffel bag full of souvenirs would ever be forwarded to me from Hsian as promised. It was, almost a year later, minus almost everything of value or interest.

I must admit I remember little of the trip back other than a brief layover in Kunming and a flight with regular seats and the warmth of a field jacket as we bounced our way over the Hump. While I must have landed in Chabua, I have no memory of it, or of going on to Calcutta. I was quite dispirited and for reasons I cannot fathom today, I had a strong sense of guilt and failure. I know I spent a very short time in bachelor officer quarters in Calcutta and was in the officers' club having a drink when the news of the bombing of Hiroshima was announced. It was received by everyone with wonder, amazement, joy, and guesstimates of how long it would be before we would be home. Several days later, possibly before the Nagasaki drop, I had boarded a Navy freighter and was on my way down the Hoogly River back to the US.

It was luxury! Even better than my previous return on the *Queen Mary*. There were about a half dozen other passengers. Surprisingly, more than half were civilians, and we all reveled in ice cream and enjoyed milk and other American fare rarely found in the CBI theater of operations, as well as vegetables (frozen) that could be enjoyed without the threat of dysentery. We had private cabins with access to an extremely varied assortment of books and games. The only cargo seemed to be a large cage located on the stern full of monkeys destined for medical research. In the meantime, the monkeys provided us with some entertainment. For us there was no other routine than that of meals, and we relaxed as we slowly sailed down the east coast of India. I had found an English literature anthology textbook that I read with curiosity in anticipation of a return to college.

It was after a week or so that we sailed into Colombo harbor and unceremoniously slammed into a stone pier at a forty-five degree angle. We spent at least the next three weeks at the dock, first waiting for arrangements to be made for repairs and then for the repairs themselves, which surprisingly involved several natives on a pontoon pounding the bow with sledgehammers to straighten it out. A section of at least five feet had to be processed in that fashion, and the fix had to be redone several times for over-corrections. Then some rivets had to be replaced and everything painted. During that time I, along with almost everybody else, spent much time ashore, both to get away from the constant hammering that resonated throughout the ship, and to see more of Ceylon. I went back to Galle for a visit, another trip to Kandy, and was invited to several parties, even a wedding reception in Colombo, the purpose of the invitation

(I imagine) being only to have another uniform present. The novelty was pleasant but, nevertheless, I was very happy when it was finally time to leave.

We continued our leisurely way around the southern tip of India, crossing the Indian Ocean into the Red Sea with a never-explained halt outside of Aden, and on up past the forbidding coast of Saudi Arabia to Suez, where we were held up several days awaiting our turn into the canal. We were not allowed off the ship either there or Port Said at the other end of the extremely slow trip across the desert, where we also stayed a day or two, probably replenishing supplies since we took on no cargo. However, there was a great deal of activity and new sights to keep us at the railings kibitzing.

The Mediterranean crossing was gentle and pleasant, and we passed through the Strait of Gibraltar one evening at dusk, after which the weather turned colder and some of the monkeys were disposed of overboard. Also disposed of in a similar fashion were quantities of ammunition for the anti-aircraft cannon and other shipboard weapons. The war was over: no sense in continuing now with the responsibility or wasted time of being accountable for all materiel issued. It could be written off with little likelihood of any query.

Sometime in late September we finally docked in Baltimore and, after some confusion and delay, I was conveyed to Washington, D.C., where I was quartered in a pyramid tent on the grounds of the Congressional Country Club. I had initially been assigned and dropped off at a WAC's barracks, obviously on the basis of my first name. It seemed damp and rainy much of the time and, while we had access to the Country Club, there was little else to do.

There we waited, I and others in the same situation, awaiting discharge. While some were waiting impatiently to get out, certain they had all the requisite points, others were trying to decide what to do next, enjoying all the while a return to quasi-civilian status. I had decided straightaway to continue my interrupted college education.

I found myself immediately dealing with several examples of bureaucracy at its worst. I spent many time-consuming and very frustrating hours in small offices where the processing of my discharge seemed to involve a detailed review of where I had been and when, the purpose of which seemed to be to account for what I had been issued. I must have spent some three days accounting for long-forgotten equipment that had been checked out to me. There was never any mention of the big items like the .32 and .45 caliber pistols, nor of the down sleeping bags issued in Burma, of all places, which I still had. Much time was spent filling out forms accounting for the sneaker-type shoes issued in Burma, which I had replaced on my own with jump boots that I had had hobnailed; an entire afternoon of discussion was spent trying to settle what had happened to the two small gold bars (*katti*) issued as emergency funds that I had turned in on leaving China, but for which I had no receipt. Fortunately, I found a catch-all footnote on one of my Chengtu papers stating that I had been properly cleared, and I finally managed to argue that surely something as important as that had been taken care of. None of this saved me from further investigation of what had happened to a machete that I had given to a Naga tribesman and even to a waterproof container for wooden matches that had ended up I had no idea where. During lunch I went to an Army-Navy store, purchased a surplus khaki waterproof match container, and rather flamboyantly dropped it on the table. To the 'So you have found it after all', I replied that I had just purchased it in a surplus store, a rejoinder that was not accepted gracefully. I was in all seriousness reprimanded for illegally disposing of government property for having given an item to a native who had helped us and for substituting one item for another. I couldn't help pointing out that the few cents I had paid for the match container and all the other minutiae we were dealing with in no way corresponded to the disposals I had been privy to at sea on my way home, and besides none of the items involved bore serial numbers. I left that group not on the best of terms, but the rest of the process went smoothly and quickly.

I was given a week's leave and my discharge papers were issued, effective, appropriately enough, the day World War I ended, 11 November 1945.

I returned to Harvard University in February and discovered that, either through charity or goodwill, my grades for that first year were not the expected 'Ds' but acceptable 'Cs' with several 'Bs' and even an 'A'. I was off to a good start and, by studying through summers, I graduated *magna cum laude* in June 1948 and began facing adult civilian life.

CHAPTER 5

'Salesman's' Prior Operations

Charles Staunton, real name Philippe Liewer, was a Parisian born and bred, married to Maryse, the daughter of a renowned medical school professor, Weil-Hallé. In the early '30s he had been a journalist for Agence Havas. In 1938 he was sent to Munich to report on that critical meeting involving Hitler, Mussolini, Daladier, and Chamberlain. The Nazis refused to let him stay and sent him back to France, I presume because he was Jewish. When the war finally started in September 1939, he served with the French forces that later were evacuated from Narvik, then became a liaison officer assigned to the British Expeditionary Force, and was evacuated with them from Dunkerque. He returned to France to say goodbye to his wife, whom he finally located in Nice. There he organized one of the first resistance groups in France. He was arrested for that activity in mid-1942 by the Vichy police and sent to a Vichy detention center, from which he escaped with some ten other prisoners in August, crossed the Pyrénées into Spain and Portugal, and succeeded in getting to England. He was recruited into SOE by Colonel Buckmaster and assumed his *nom de guerre* of Charles Staunton.

After completing the usual training, less the parachute jumps, he was landed by Lysander in March 1943 near Blois with the mission of organizing resistance in the Rouen area, the first operation called 'Salesman'. With the help of Serge Malraux (brother of the famous writer André Malraux), he formed a large underground resistance organization centered in Le Havre comprising many small independent cells and circuits. In April a radio operator called Peter Newman was flown in by Lysander, and through him arms and explosives were dropped in, along with a fully trained weapons and demolitions instructor named Bob Mortier, real name Bob Maloubier.

Bob was born in Paris in 1923, the second son of parents who had lived in New York. His father had taught at Columbia, and his older brother was a US citizen, having been born in New York. He attended the Lycée Pasteur, not an exceptional student, was more interested in the sports activities of the Racing Club to which his parents had gotten him a membership so that he could correct the damage caused to his legs by bad burns from the carelessness of a maid when he was two.

The war did nothing to encourage scholarship, and the *lycée* closed due to the war shortly before Bob was to take his baccalaureate exams, so he never graduated from the *lycée*. With what little financial help his parents could spare, he headed south to get to England.

After several unsuccessful attempts (hidden under luggage and clothing in the back seat of an American friend's car), he got past the French border only to get caught and turned back by the Spanish authorities. At Saint-Jean-de-Luz, where remnants of the Polish army were embarking, he accepted the offer of a spare uniform from a Polish corporal but was turned back on the gangplank when unable to respond when spoken to in Polish. He worked his way over to Marseilles, where he managed to subsist as a bar keeper with an interim round trip to Paris in the occupied zone with a friend who wanted to remove his weapons collection from his parents' home, fearing the difficulties it might cause if discovered.

Then in early 1941, when the Pétain regime began forming a new French army, he and a friend volunteered for the Air Force with the intention of flying to England their first solo flight. He ended up at a fighter base in Bizerte, Tunisia, which had no planes available. When on leave he tried crossing again into the occupied zone for Christmas in Paris, was caught and, unable to return for duty, was classified AWOL, eventually ending up in the brig in Bizerte until released in the summer. To counter reversals at El Alamein and Allied landings in Morocco, the Germans took over Tunisia with French compliance, at which time Bob and a friend stole two bicycles, one belonging to his colonel, and rode several hundred kilometers into Algeria, dodging French and German troops. There they met up with the advance elements of a British force just as it was being bombed. They helped as liaison with necessary civilian medical help, but refused to stay with the British, stating that they wanted to get to England to fly. Given passes to Algiers, little by little Bob became aware of a Gaullist group with British sponsorship. When a close friend of his shot Admiral Darlan, and the police wanted to question him, he sought refuge with that group, was recruited by de Guélis on the understanding that it was not to become a fighter pilot, and was put on a corvette to Gibraltar. From there they reached England by convoy and Bob was picked up by SOE. By June 1943 he had completed his training (weapons, sabotage, industrial demolition, general clandestine operations) but had had to wait until the August moon to parachute in after several unsuccessful attempts. So it was on 15 August that he dropped into Staunton's network as the replacement of a Canadian saboteur, Gaby Chartrand, who managed to escape the Gestapo to England.

He and Staunton worked closely and well together. From then until December Bob trained and led his group in many operations, the most effective being the sinking of a submarine tender which had managed to avoid the blockade of the Royal Navy, eliciting the popular joke 'How clever these Germans are. They hide their boats under water so to protect them from the RAF.' Bob was also responsible for the sabotage of a factory manufacturing Focke-Wulf airplane parts, and seriously damaging and immobilizing the largest electricity generating plant, which sustained much of the industry in the Rouen area. Staunton continued organizing his groups in preparation for the invasion that was obviously coming and gathering information on German efforts around Le Havre.

By early December, prior to leaving by Lysander to return for consultation in England, Staunton suggested to Bob that he take the group's forger along at the next drop, both as a reward for his excellent work and to satisfy his curiosity. For some reason the truck that was to carry the materiel from the DZ did not show up, and Bob and the forger took a motorcycle to notify the reception group. They just managed to leave Rouen before curfew. A short time later they were stopped by a police car. The forger ran and got away. Bob was forced to take the motorcycle to a local police station, a German sitting behind him with a drawn pistol. As they approached the police station, the police car that had been following them passed. Bob saw his chance and went into a sharp skid, throwing off the German; he threw the motorcycle at him and ran down a side street as the policeman shot at him and started to pursue him. He was shot through the lungs but managed to cross a canal, thus leaving no scent for the dogs that were trailing him, and collapsed unconscious and soaking wet in a field in below-zero temperatures.

At dawn he found he was still alive and somehow managed the seventeen kilometers to Rouen to his friends' apartment. Dr Delbos, the network physician, didn't have much hope and discussions were held as to how best to dispose of Bob's body. The final solution, to tie his ankles to his shoulders before rigor mortis set in so that he would fit into a couple of potato sacks sewn together, was never executed. Sulfa drugs were dropped in and he recovered. He returned to England by Hudson bomber in February along with Staunton, whose Lysander had failed to materialize in December, as had several January departures.

Eager to get back and avoid the frequent delays of travel by Lysander, Staunton went to Jump School, where he met Violette Szabó, who was finishing her jump training after having hurt her ankle. Staunton chose her to accompany him, and they and Bob spent considerable time together while Bob was recuperating from his wound, which he survived, it turned out, because the extreme cold of his night in the field cauterized his internal wounds.

Violette Szabó, née Violette Reine Bushell, was born in Paris on 26 June 1921. Her mother, Reine Leroy, had met her father, Charles Bushell, when he was serving in France and they had married in Reine's hometown of Pont-Rémy in northern France at the end of World War I. The family, comprised of Violette's older brother Roy, born in 1920, and two younger brothers, John and Noel, born in 1924 and 1926 respectively, had lived for periods in both France and England as Charles worked different jobs, mostly self-employment. In 1926 the family moved to Pont-Rémy before finally returning on a more permanent basis to England in 1929, though Violette and one of her brothers normally went to stay with their mother's relatives in France for several weeks every summer, as well as spending much other time with her aunt in Wormelow, Herefordshire. In addition, Violette had five male cousins a little older than she with whom she played. By all accounts she was a tomboy and more than held her own. She did well in school, though she was never really interested in reading and books. She was more at ease in French than English when they first returned to England. She left school when she was about fifteen, enjoying work as a shop girl in various stores. She barely made it back to England from the summer vacation in France when the war started in 1939.

She joined the land army for a short time, helping with harvests. At her mother's suggestion, on 14 July 1940, the French national holiday, she brought home a French Foreign Legion Lieutenant who had just been evacuated from Narvik. His name was Étienne Szabó, he was eleven years older than she, and it was love at first sight. They were married within three weeks. In 1941 he got seven days' leave from Africa, possibly with the influence of General Koenig, who had been his captain in the Legion before he rowed across the Channel and was promoted to General by de Gaulle. In September 1941, Violette joined the ATS and trained and worked in an anti-aircraft battery until April 1942, when she left due to her pregnancy.

Their daughter, Tania, was born 8 June 1942. Although she was not notified for several months, Étienne died of wounds received at El Alamein in October 1942.

Shortly after receiving the news of Étienne's death, Violette was recruited by SOE and received clandestine training at Wanborough Manor, weapons training at Arisaig, intelligence at Beaulieu, and parachute training at Ringway. She badly sprained her ankle before finishing the course. It was at the end of a later course in early March 1944 that she met Staunton. He was impressed by her and convinced Colonel Buckmaster that she should be the one to act as intermediary with the Rouen network and the Le Havre area, which was closed to all except residents since the field had notified London that both he and Bob were known to the Germans. According to her false papers, Violette became Mlle Corinne Reine Leroy. They were scheduled to parachute in during the March moon, but the very afternoon they were to leave a message from someone named Catherine, who claimed to be a friend of Malraux, reported from Nice that the Rouen network had been captured and that the Germans had been using Peter Newman's codes in the hope of being their reception committee. The team's departure was stopped literally at the very end of the runway. Several weeks later, they finally flew in by Lysander and were dropped near Chartres.

The mission now was to determine the status of the network and what remained that might still be operational. Leaving Staunton to oversee other pre-invasion operations, three days after her arrival, Violette took the train to Rouen and began the delicate and dangerous task of contacting people she did not know except by descriptions from Staunton, trying to casually use the password previously in use, hoping for recognition and contact. She was to meet Staunton in Paris by the end of April. By then she had determined that of the ninety-eight network members only eight had not been taken. She also managed to spend some time in Le Havre to report on some of the fortifications the Germans were building. When she recontacted Staunton in Paris, he realized that nothing could be expected of the Rouen group and told her to recontact him in three days. She did some shopping during that interval and in early May they returned to England by Lysander. It was about three weeks later that I became involved with the three of them.

POSTSCRIPTS

Violette Szabó

After her capture, as I discovered much later, she was sent to Fresnes prison just outside Paris, and was there some seven weeks, during which time she was interrogated in the Gestapo headquarters at 84 Avenue Foch. In early August, shortly before the liberation of Paris, she was sent to the Ravensbruck concentration camp just north of Berlin. Three weeks later she, Denise Bloch and Lillian Rolfe, two captured SOE radio operators, were sent to Torgau, a work camp located about two hundred kilometers south of Ravensbruck. By October the three women were sent to Königsberg, another work camp. In January, as the Allies were closing in from both east and west, the three were returned to Ravensbruck, where they were shot. In 1946, Vera Atkins traced down Violette's last days and identified and prosecuted the two men responsible for her death: Fritz Suhren and Johann Schwarzhuber were hanged.

Philippe Liewer aka Charles Staunton

I know very little of what happened to Staunton after the end of 'Salesman'. He went back to England, and apparently was thinking of moving to Canada since he asked SOE to deposit his checks in a Canadian bank. In 1946 he was back in France and seems to have separated from his wife. He was living with a mistress when Maloubier saw him again in late August of that year and had written a book entitled *Voyageurs au Claire de Lune*, a story about espionage no doubt based on his own experiences. Apparently the mistress ended up with the manuscript, which seems to have disappeared. He later moved to North Africa, and died of pneumonia in Tunisia in the mid-1950s.

Bob Maloubier

When we separated in Paris in October 1944, I had Bob's address since I had stayed at his parents' apartment in Neuilly. We corresponded twice when I was in China and after that we were both busy with our own activities. He, too, was offered a mission in Germany, but instead joined Force 136, a commando group set up by SOE that ended up in Annam after training in Ceylon. The group seems to have been transferred to French control when General De Lattre de Tassigny was sent to Indochina. Bob was appointed acting governor of the province of Thanh Hoa, had a terrible campaign, ambushed by both Chinese and Viet forces, had his *maquis compagnon* Jacques Dufour (Anastasie) die in his arms, and finally returned in August 1946 suffering badly from malaria. The next thirteen years were spent with a new French intelligence service with paramilitary ambitions, the DGER. He was one of four persons in charge of setting up a paramilitary parachute battalion (the *onzième de choc*), followed by forming a frogman unit which turned out to be so successful in training demonstrations against the French Navy that the navy took it over. He then did a stint in Austria surveying targets (tunnels, power plants and the like) to see which, if sabotaged with explosives, would most effectively immobilize the country should it be occupied by the Russians. He also set up and directed a training school for Central Europeans to be infiltrated into the Soviet Union. His final assignment involved overseeing the attempted assassinations of North African leaders in revolt against France, during which time he and the Service became involved with the French mafia, and his boss asked him to disappear (with full salary) to Montevideo until things cleared up. Instead, at the last minute, he flew with his wife Nicole to Leopoldville, Congo. When word reached them that he should return to France, he decided he had had enough and resigned.

He found a job running lumber camps deep in the wilds of Gabon and, after two years, went to work for Shell in Lagos. Nicole and he divorced about that time and from then on he worked for various French oil companies, with an intermediate hitch establishing and running the security forces of the president of Gabon, where he met his second wife Catherine. He was also involved in the Biafran war (on the Nigerian side) and went all over the Middle East with the French Elf oil company, struggling to put up with the formal bureaucracy: Lebanon in 1975, during the long civil war; and Cairo, Kuwait, Tripoli, Djedda, Riyad, Oman, Qatar and Ankara at other periods. He quit in the early '80s, to live on a small estate that Catherine owned near Moulins and an apartment in Paris. He has written several books and is active in the memorial ceremonies for Second World War clandestine operations. I saw him again for the first time since 1944 at the opening of the Violette Szabó Museum in Wormelow, Herefordshire in June 2000. We had an excellent session which, I hope, will be repeated.

AFTERWORD BY
CLAUDIA ALICE HOLZER

Upon his discharge in November 1945, Jean Claude returned to Harvard. He was gratified to learn that he received some science, math and chemistry credits for his experiences with explosives, demolition, cartography and cryptography. He was a member of the Speakers Club. In 1948, he received a Master of Arts *magna cum laude* in Romance languages and literature. During this time he met Gertrude Alice Flaherty – known as Alice – in the Boston Commons. She was a student at Boston University and had recently been honourably discharged from the US Coast Guard. She was very intelligent and beautiful and they fell in love. They planned to marry when Jean Claude graduated. However, his mother did not approve of the match. Alice's family was not in the Social Register and she was from North Adams, Massachusetts, a mill town! Jeanne forbade Jean Claude from marrying Alice but, for the first time in his life, with support from his brother Pierre, he defied his mother.

Jean Claude and Alice were married on 21 August 1948 in the First Church at Cambridge. His parents did not attend the wedding. Pierre was the best man. Jean Claude and Alice would be partners for life. They honeymooned in Nantucket and settled in Ipswich,

Massachusetts in a large house owned by Jean Claude's parents. Pierre, his wife Velvin and their young son Philippe also lived there and Jean Claude's parents spent extended periods there too. It was not an ideal arrangement but necessary because Jean Claude's mother refused to relinquish the army pay he had sent home for her to save for him.

After a short while, Jean Claude and Alice moved back to Northampton. Jean Claude was able to secure a job in New York City which meant he had to commute back and forth. He stayed with his Tante Margot and Oncle Lorenzo in their NYC apartment during the week and spent the weekends in Northampton. It was difficult for Alice but they needed his salary. Jean Claude took a teaching position in the French department at New York University, instructing students who were not much younger than he was.

In July 1949, Jean Claude and Alice's first child, myself, Claudia Alice, was born. Several months later, they moved to Columbus, Ohio, where Jean Claude taught French at Ohio State University. They lived in an old farmhouse with a large garden and a cat. Jean Claude grew a lot of their food since a new professor's salary was barely adequate. But they were happy and free from his domineering mother. Their second child, Daniel Claude, was born in July 1951.

In 1953, the family moved to Oxen Hill, Maryland, where Jean Claude had some association or connection with the OSS/CIA in Washington, D.C. This is a grey area that he never discussed but in 1954 the family was shipped overseas to Saipan, an island in the South Pacific. Jean Claude had the choice of being shipped to Beirut, Lebanon or Saipan. They chose Saipan perhaps in part due to the fact that his mother would never be able to travel there, while she might make it to Beirut! On Saipan, the family lived in a Quonset hut on the army base. Jean Claude drove us all over the island in an army jeep. There were remnants of the bloody battles the US fought against the Japanese who held control over the island until the Marines prevailed. There was a rusted, bombed-out destroyer in the lagoon as well as shell-scarred cliffs from which the Japanese soldiers' families jumped or were thrown to their deaths when it became obvious that the Americans would take the island.

Saipan was a beautiful tropical island with coconut palms, banana trees, hibiscus, frangipanis and sugar cane. It had dense jungles with a wide variety of animals and insects. On the beaches were giant sea turtles, crabs, sea urchins and incredible sea shells. It was safe in the lagoon but beyond the reef the water was dangerous. The ocean was rough and sharks were plentiful. Jean Claude once took his children and a friend sailing outside the reef and were circled by several sharks. He had his army-issue pistol but did not use it. From the lagoon side of the reef, Jean Claude dove down and cut some coral (something that would never be done today). His family still has the sea shells and coral from their time on the island. At Christmas, Santa Claus parachuted out of a helicopter and handed out gifts to the children on the base.

From Saipan, the family travelled to Tinian (where the two planes carrying the atomic bombs that would level Hiroshima and Nagasaki took off), Guam, Wake Island, Iwo Jima, Okinawa, Japan and the Philippines. Post Second World War, destruction and rebuilding were evident in all these locations. Even though they travelled as a family, Jean Claude occasionally disappeared to meet up with unknown individuals. Two Filipino fishermen loaded him into a dugout canoe and disappeared for hours. It was rumoured that the intelligence community on Saipan was involved in some sort of front-end work on the eventual overthrow of the Diem regime in Viet Nam. Jean Claude never discussed this and I don't know if it can be verified. It is logical that his experience with the OSS and his facility with the French language would have been useful in French Indochina.

Like so many veterans, Jean Claude was reticent to discuss his Second World War experiences. Growing up, his children knew that he kept his original papers, medals and other artefacts such as lock-picking tools (rakes), a wallet with secret compartments, silk code sheets and maps in an old tin bread box. On rare occasions, he would show us some of his artefacts. He was very humble when he talked about his medals or his service. He would talk in generalities of what a wireless operator did, how he learned Morse code and how all-important the crystals were to his radio. He told his children that the silk code sheets could easily be swallowed if necessary. This intrigued his children and they wondered what silk tasted like. He never mentioned the danger or the short life expectancy of a wireless operator (six weeks). Jean Claude made his parachute jumping experiences sound like fun. Again, there was no mention of the danger or the mission. Other than these rare occasions, his SOE/OSS activities and experiences remained in his memory and the tangible artefacts in the bread box. It would be years before his children learned the greater story. We were told to say that he worked for the State Department, if asked.

Returning stateside in 1956, the family landed in San Francisco and drove cross-country visiting many national parks on the way back to Washington, D.C. The Plymouth station wagon, which had been shipped to Saipan and back, was waiting for them in San Francisco. The family initially settled in Baltimore, Maryland, where Jean Claude had associations with Defense Department contractors. In 1957, the family moved to Falls Church, Virginia, and in 1958, moved down the road to Arlington. They lived a few blocks away from John Glenn, the first American to orbit the Earth.

In 1961, Jean Claude was hired by Honeywell International as a program manager. His job was to negotiate for Defense Department contracts. The family moved to Minneapolis, Minnesota, where the winters were brutally cold. He taught his children how to ice skate, ice fish, sled, toboggan and make snow forts. He set up an HO gauge train on the basement ping pong table. He refused to buy the pre-made buildings, autos or trees and made his own by hand. The trees were composed of some unknown organic matter and he built the autos and buildings using balsa wood, plastic wrap, sand paper and whatever material seemed to work. Jean Claude was a very attentive parent who took great delight in his children's development. Perhaps due to his sheltered childhood, he wanted to ensure that theirs would be different. He rode the rollercoaster with us; he taught us how to swim; he was waiting in the deep end of the pool when we jumped off the high diving board; he helped us with our homework and school projects; he encouraged us to have hobbies; he hiked and biked with us; he taught us how to drive; he gave us a crystal radio set and showed us how to assemble it; he taught us how to plant and grow vegetables. He gave much of himself to his family.

In 1963, Honeywell transferred the family to Clearwater, Florida. Jean Claude and Alice became active in the Civil Rights movement and they made sure that their children understood that segregation was terribly wrong. They were exposed to segregated schools, restaurants, water fountains, hotels, clubs, restrooms and to the hatred that some people exuded. Jean Claude would dutifully drop off his children at the Unitarian Church (which was also involved with the Civil Rights movement) for Sunday school. He waited in the car for two hours reading the *New York Times*.

Honeywell transferred the family back to Minneapolis, Minnesota in 1965. Jean Claude and his children built a fourteen-foot long sailboat in their garage during another frigid winter. He taught them how to use tools and follow written directions. Some enjoyable time was spent going to hardware stores.

In 1967, Jean Claude's brother Pierre was killed in an automobile accident in Ripon, Wisconsin. His death was devastating for Jean Claude and for Pierre's wife Velvin and his two sons, Philippe and Michel.

In 1968, Honeywell transferred the family out west to Denver, Colorado. The family settled in Observatory Park near the University of Denver. They would walk to the Student Union and watch old movies like Laurel and Hardy. Jean Claude would laugh so hard that other moviegoers would laugh at him. Jean Claude and Alice made some very close friends here. One of their neighbours had an incredibly annoying little dog that barked hysterically whenever Jean Claude mowed the grass next to the fence. Jean Claude would let loose a stream of French swearing at the dog. One day, the neighbour came to Jean Claude's door, introduced herself and said she wanted to meet the person who swore so exquisitely in French. It turned out that she was a French professor at the University of Denver! On the weekends, the family enjoyed exploring the beautiful Rocky Mountains going on hikes, picnics and discovering log cabins in the woods.

On 7 September 1977, Jean Claude's father René died of a heart attack in Northampton, Massachusetts. A few years later, his mother, Jeanne, moved to Denver to be near the family. She died on 23 May 1989.

Jean Claude retired from Honeywell in 1986 and travelled widely with Alice. He pursued his hobby of collecting stamps and had an impressive and fairly valuable collection. Sadly, it was stolen during a robbery of their home along with his coin collection. During their retirement, they lived in Santa Barbara, California; Prescott, Arizona; Tucson, Arizona; Newport, Oregon; and Denver, Colorado. Again, they made some very close friends in these locations. They enjoyed travelling throughout the US, Canada, Mexico, the Caribbean and Europe. Another of Jean Claude's great pleasures was food. He loved it all and could indulge a huge appetite without putting on weight. He was especially fond of sweets, particularly semi-sweet dark chocolate. But he also enjoyed roasts of beef, lamb, pork, chicken or whatever. When he carved and had access to the bones, there was not one shred of meat left on them nor any marrow left in them. He was like a scavenger and the carcass looked like an archaeological remain.

In 1987, Jean Claude suffered a heart attack while visiting family in Durango, Colorado. He was rushed to the emergency room and stabilised enough for him to be transported by air ambulance to a heart centre in Albuquerque, New Mexico. Alice was seated next to the pilot in the cockpit for the flight. She clearly heard Jean Claude's voice from the back say, 'Don't let her touch a thing up there!' It made everyone feel more optimistic! He had an angiogram and an angioplasty and recovered fully with some medication and diet changes.

Jean Claude began to write his memoir in 1994 at the age of 70. At that time, he and Alice lived in Tucson, Arizona. In 2000, he travelled to England for the opening of the Violette Szabó Museum in Wormelow, Herefordshire. He met up with Robert Maloubier for the first time since the liberation of Paris and met Leo Marks for the first time in person. He had been on the receiving end of Jean Claude's radio transmissions. It was an emotional reunion for all of them.

In 2001, Jean Claude and Alice visited France and explored the Jura district. They travelled throughout the area where the 'Salesman' circuit had operated, including Sussac and Limoges. According to Jean Claude, they located a few veterans of the *maquis* who remembered him. Jean Claude had a memory of a water wheel near his broadcast site that had been used to produce electricity, which ran a small generator and made him independent of the local power supply. One of the veterans did remember a water wheel but it had long since been destroyed. Robert Maloubier joined them and spent time reminiscing. This was an important and emotional trip for Jean Claude.

Jean Claude and Alice spent long summers in Newport, Oregon. They were very close to the harbour and Jean Claude had his sailboat (newer and larger than the one he had built years ago in his garage) moored at the marina. Newport had a working harbour and the fishing boats brought in fresh fish daily. Japanese ships loaded up lumber to return to Japan. It was a fascinating place to be. They met their summer neighbours, who would become the closest of friends for years. Their two grandsons visited for a month every summer. Jean Claude taught them how to sail and how to catch, clean and cook Dungeness crab from Newport Bay. He taught them chess and other games. He taught them how to fly two-stringed stunt kites on the windy Pacific beaches of Newport. He took great pleasure in his grandchildren and great-grandchildren.

While spending their first summer in Newport, Oregon, it became quickly evident that there was terrible radio reception except for the small local AM station. Alice enjoyed listening to the radio and wanted a greater selection of stations. Jean Claude bought some antenna wire, tied a rock around one end and had his grandsons hold the other end. He threw the rock up and over a very tall pine tree (just as the OSS had trained him!). The antenna wire ended up anchored high up in the tree. The other end was slipped through the kitchen window and attached to Alice's radio. She received stations from all along the west coast and especially enjoyed one from San Francisco!

While travelling through Astoria, Washington, where the Columbia River meets the Pacific Ocean, Jean Claude and family stopped to look at a large Russian freighter moored there. Some crewmen invited us onboard and in the control room an officer was sending and receiving messages in Morse code. One of Jean Claude's grandsons said, 'That's what you did, grandpa'. The Russians sat him down and put headphones on him and he sent a Morse code message to someone somewhere and received an answering message. He said it was about the weather.

Jean Claude was a man of many facets. He was a keen observer of detail and remained so almost to the end of his life. He was a master improviser who successfully utilised what was at hand. He was resourceful, meticulous and creative. He could blend in with any group of people like a chameleon. He could speak intelligently on a wide range of topics. He had amazing energy and resilience. Many people believed that he was a 'social animal' but really he was quite reclusive. He could perform beautifully in social situations, but most of the time it was not easy or enjoyable for him. He was always happy to retire to quiet. People thought of him as a gentleman, which he was.

However, he could also be quite negative about the human race. He believed that a benevolent dictator was the solution to many situations. His humour tended to be on the dark side. He believed in the French adage that 'laws are made to be bypassed', which was exemplified by his 'creativity' when completing his federal income tax forms. Every year, his family feared an audit, a fine or even jail time (jail never happened!). If he thought that a law was unnecessary or stupid then he had no obligation to follow it. He thus accumulated a huge number of speeding and parking tickets. Alice did not take these transgressions well. He could lie with ease if a situation required it. He could be unpredictable and impulsive in his actions, as when he chased down and tripped up a purse snatcher who was much younger and bigger than he was. He was a law unto himself many times over.

Jean Claude and Alice moved back to Denver permanently in 2007. In 2010, he was diagnosed with Alzheimer's. Not too surprisingly, the few memories that remained with him were of the war. In the last two years of his life, he began to transpose car licence plates into Morse code. Whenever we were stopped at a signal, he would 'dit, dot, dit' the licence number of the car in front of us. I confess that it was annoying but impressive! On 2 July 2012, Jean Claude lost his wife of sixty-three years. He was very confused and could never understand or accept that Alice was dead. He could not live alone or independently, so the difficult decision was made to move him into an assisted living facility nearby. For a brief period, he seemed to adjust. But then he would wander off the grounds and get lost. Shortly thereafter, he was placed in a 'secured area'. It was a locked-down wing which had a keypad that allowed staff and family to enter or leave using a code. No resident knew the code. Claudia and her husband Joe began to receive calls from the facility saying that Jean Claude was 'missing'. He had managed to escape from the locked-down area. Once, he just tagged along behind a family as they were leaving, pretending that he also had just visited someone, saying, 'I'll just follow you out'. He was returned at 3 a.m. Then he figured that if he hung out near the keypad, he might be able to see the code that people put in! That worked very well for him and he made a few more successful escapes. If he hadn't been my father, I might have been very amused by his cleverness, but I wasn't and neither was the facility since they had to repeatedly change their codes in an effort to thwart his escapes. The final straw came when I was at the nurses' station speaking with his nurse and we both looked up to see him standing in the open 'secure' doorway. He said to hurry before the alarm sounded in ten seconds. So, he had figured out another code and now knew he only had ten seconds to escape before the staff were alerted. The writing was on the wall. The facility could not allow him to remain a resident, for his safety and their liability. Jean Claude moved into Claudia and Joe's house in late 2012. He was comfortable, happy and secure in this setting. There were no more escape attempts. His Alzheimer's progressed rapidly, as did other health issues. He died on 22 March 2013. His last words were, 'I wonder how many miles I've ridden on trains.'

Both Jean Claude and Alice were 89 when they died and their remains are interred at Fort Logan National Cemetery in Denver. The Silver Star is listed on Jean Claude's headstone. His was a life well lived!

ACKNOWLEDGEMENTS

I am deeply indebted to my agent, Mark H. Yeats, for his practical guidance and his vast knowledge of and passion for all things SOE/OSS. His remarkable patience and professionalism was evident at every step of the process. He recognised my father's memoir as a story that needed to be told and made it all possible.

I thank my editor, Chrissy McMorris at The History Press, who brought this endeavour to fruition with intelligence and sensitivity.

My deepest appreciation to Tania Szabó for writing her very thoughtful foreword to this book, for referring me to her agent Mark Yeats and for her kind support.

I am also very grateful to Robert Maloubier for his amazing foreword and for sharing experiences that illuminate my father as a young man.

I owe a great deal to Julie and Ron La Point for their deep personal interest in my father's story and their assistance to him with word processing. My father referred to his computer as 'that damned infernal machine'.

I am also thankful to Robert Forte, who has a great knowledge of the wireless radio that my father used and strongly supported the publication of this memoir.

INDEX

If you enjoyed this book, you may also be interested in…

Young, Brave and Beautiful

TANIA SZABÓ

978 0 7509 6209 4

SOE agent Violette Szabó was one of the most incredible women who operated behind enemy lines during the Second World War. The daughter of an English father and French mother, and widow of a French army officer, she was daring and courageous, conducting sabotage missions, being embroiled in gun battles and battling betrayal. On her second mission she was captured by the Nazis, interrogated and tortured, then deported to Germany where she was eventually executed at Ravensbrück concentration camp. Violette was one of the first women ever to be awarded the George Cross, and her fascinating life has been immortalised in film and on the page. Written by her daughter, *Young, Brave and Beautiful* reveals the woman and mother behind this extraordinary hero.

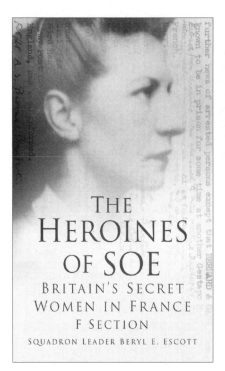

The Heroines of SOE

SQUADRON LEADER BERYL
E. ESCOTT

978 0 7524 8729 8

'They were the war's bravest women, devoted to defeating the Nazis yet reluctant ever to reveal their heroic pasts. Now a new book tells their intrepid tales.' *Daily Express*

Britain's war in the shadows of male spies and subterfuge in the heart of occupied France is a story well known, but what of the women who also risked their lives for Britain and the liberation of France? In 1942 a desperate need for new recruits saw SOE turn to a previously overlooked group – women. These extraordinary women came from different backgrounds, but were joined in their idealistic love of France and a desire to play a part in its liberation. They formed SOE's F Section. From the famous White Mouse, Nancy Wake, to the courageous Noor Inayat Khan, they all risked their lives for King, Country and the Resistance. Many of them died bravely and painfully, and often those who survived, like Eileen Nearne, never told their stories, yet their secret missions of intelligence-gathering and sabotage undoubtedly helped the Resistance to drive out their occupiers and free France. Here, for the first time, is the extraordinary account of all forty SOE F women agents. It is a story that deserves to be read by everyone. Squadron Leader Beryl E. Escott served in the RAF and is one of the foremost experts on the women of SOE.

Visit our website and discover thousands of other History Press books.

www.thehistorypress.co.uk